OTHER BOOKS BY LISA HOBBS:

*I Saw Red China*

*India, India*

# LOVE AND LIBERATION

# LOVE
## AND
# LIBERATION

[Up Front with the Feminists]

*by  Lisa Hobbs*

McGRAW-HILL BOOK COMPANY

New York    St. Louis    San Francisco    Düsseldorf
London    Mexico    Sydney    Toronto

Library of Congress Catalog Card Number: 79-139554

SECOND PRINTING

07-029093-8

*To J.E.H.*

# LOVE AND LIBERATION

# CHAPTER

# I

Last fall I was at a Midwestern university lecturing on the People's Republic of China. A press interview followed. At its conclusion, and as an afterthought, one of the newsmen asked with a grin, "What do you think about this new craze women are on?"

They all smiled at me. My lecture had been analytic; there was no danger I could be one of "them."

I asked why he had used the word "craze." There was no reply. Smiles faded and the men started to leave in silence. Then, drifting from the hall in a deliberately loud voice, came the judgment:

"Another broad who needs a . . ."

I am a woman. I have loved and hated. Been seduced and have seduced. Have been the giver of love and the taker of love. Shed tears and caused tears. Given pleasure and received pain. Given pain and received pleasure. Have loved black and hated white. Have loved white and hated black. I have borne two sons in pain and given them milk from my body with love.

I am a woman. But a woman in a man's world.

This means that my life thus far has been spent living within institutions and concepts which men, not women, made. It means that I must act, feel, look and speak in ways which man has determined are "suitable" for me. These modes of behavior were determined thousands of years ago when woman, lacking any means of birth control, was condemned to live her life within a narrow and limiting biological context. They have survived because man established his "manhood" in direct proportion to his ability to override the female and sustains his ego-strength through this process. Taking stock of this biological difference, he has exploited it by initiating and supporting institutions and attitudes that gave the male ego an almost supreme power over the female ego. These institutions and attitudes remain intact today and it is the aim of the women's liberation movement to destroy them.

Among my more radical sisters there are some who do not count me as a feminist, for I use the word *love* too often. Too many of my sisters have found, in their personal as well as their business lives, that to earn the sweets of male love and approval, they have had to surrender their souls. Small wonder that they loathe the word. My experiences in this respect have not been identical with theirs, thanks to my good fortune in being married to a liberated man. But as for male hate—that special poison that the male glands manufacture when confronted with an intelligent and ambitious woman—there is nothing that the most radical feminist could teach me. I have been living feminism daily for twenty years and that means twenty years of open and guerrilla warfare. Imagine, for instance, male reaction to me—a wife of nineteen years and mother of two children—hopping around Vietnam in a gunship as a reporter! How the male adrenalin flowed on that one! It was most satisfying. For what I could see as my male critics jumped around swinging their verbal clubs were mental primates in gray flannel suits, primates who are so locked into their fossilized perceptions of the female that they cannot see, let alone understand, the changes that are shifting and swelling all around them. When they manage to stop swinging, they will be in for a shock. They will find themselves confronting a new woman—not a flirtatious virgin, passive wife or grateful girlfriend—but a brand-new woman who will place her human rights in the forefront of her demands, a woman who will be willing to fight for them.

This book is concerned primarily with the American woman, as she is the woman I know best. I have been living, laughing, arguing, crying and swapping ideas with her for the last twenty years. Yet she is not so much different from women anywhere in Western society. A little more raucous, perhaps, because she refuses to efface herself and consequently is more frustrated. Wherever I go in Western society, I see women experiencing to a greater or less degree the same psychological oppression that dominates the American woman's life. I do not need European, Canadian, American, English and Australian women's magazines to tell me that women can no longer quite cope with being women. I need no help from the mass media to realize that women are living their lives in an increasing aura of ambivalence, perplexity and frustration. I am as much a recipient as any woman of the messages society is sending me. If I do not feel perplexed and abandoned, it is not because I am less female but simply because I am more liberated, and, honesty compels me to say, fortunate enough to have had my children in a time when bearing babies was considered socially constructive and not socially destructive.

This brings us to the heart of the so-called "woman problem"—the prime reason why docile, passive and subjugated woman is ripe for revolutionary changes within her life. *Large numbers of children are no longer needed to maintain the human species. Woman's sole societal function, so long held in awe and veneration, has become a cursed, destructive power. The only feminine role that was socially imperative and unique to the female genetic nature has lost its societal value. Our bodies are now obsolete in an overpopulated world.* Our wombs in which children should grow, the passage through which we should thrust them, the breasts with which we should feed them—all our once precious female attributes are as valuable as scrap in the auto junkyard.

Those of us who live in literate nations are being fed this message daily. True, we go on having babies; for thousands of years we have had nothing better to do. Our programming cannot be switched off overnight. And so we are split in two. Our whole lives as women demand that we reproduce. But our bodies and our programming are anachronisms. They cry for fulfillment in a society that is already swaying under a load of dirty air, monstrous freeways, paper-box housing, disintegrating schools, public hospitals run like evacuation centers—all pervaded by the fears and terrors that are generated when one man is laid on top of another ad infinitum.

Not for a minute am I denying the deep and authentic joy of motherhood, or the rich satisfaction of seeing one's own little sprout grow into a beautiful young man or woman—although it should be noted here that traditional images to the contrary, not all loving women experience this pleasure. I am saying that these pleasures are minuscule compared to the forces working in the opposite direction; and I am saying that the pleasures and the satisfactions of parenthood have been exaggerated out of all proportion.

The woman with teenagers faces these realities daily; there is nothing in our whole female experience that could have adequately prepared us for motherhood in these times. When we gave birth—or I should say planned to be impregnated—it was for any number of reasons. We had a baby because we were married and married women had babies. Or perhaps we were among those few women to whom a baby is actually a joy and an act of creation. Maybe we thought a baby would strengthen a weak marriage. Or had a baby reluctantly because the masculine ego demanded that we prove our husbands were "real" men, or that we were "real" women. Or perhaps our aging parents, or his, produced a pressure too subtle to fight. Or perhaps we wanted to build ourselves an empire and hogtie our man to us for the term of his natural life. Or perhaps, and hopefully, we loved our man, loved to be with him that way, craved to carry part of him within us and reproduce part of him into the world.

Whatever our reasons, when we were impregnated ten or fifteen years ago accidentally or otherwise, it was a Good

Thing. We were acting out our historic and generic role as perpetuator of the species. Today we look out into a world in which our children have become burdensome population statistics. We have increased and multiplied as bidden and every day we are told that by the year 2000 there will be six billion people on the face of the earth and already one-third of those in existence go to bed hungry every night.

The forces bearing down on my younger sister bring with them an even more bitter comprehension. Her body is still equipped with womb, vagina and breasts. The need to reproduce at least once has been driven into her psyche like a nail. The only dream that has been offered her—the large house in the suburbs with its big station wagon, washing machine, dryer—demands that she reproduce, for without children all these material goods are meaningless. But if she is literate, she cannot escape the knowledge that every mouth she brings into the world could take life from a mouth already in existence. That's the worst of it. The best of it is the knowledge that she does not as yet require a license from the state giving her permission to have a baby, as she will in the future.

It is important then to understand that this revolution in our world is not a result of any effort on man's part to better our lives nor is it the result of a spontaneous explosion within the modern female psyche. It is science that is precipitating this revolution, science with both its life-giving gifts and deadly by-products. Science has taken from us our only role of any value and by so doing is forcing us to alter the historic course of our lives from one of biological subservience to that of full equality. Men are not doing this:

most are still fossilized within an obsolete ideology in which woman's biological nature takes precedence over all other aspects of her nature. There is ample evidence of the destruction such men cause by their pathetic inability to grow and change with the growing, changing world: they stem and crush female talent in their professional lives; their self-righteousness drives their daughters away; their wives, burdened by the false imagery that these men demand women fulfill, keep their reality hidden and spend their lives mouthing the scripts they have written. As the revolution accelerates, this clinging to a biological view of woman will cause not only great anguish but a further crystallization of the male need for supremacy.

We too will suffer, for in order to reach our maximum human growth it will be necessary to deny and oppose all authority in which we do not believe. This means that traditional male-female relationships, including traditional marriage, are destined for the fire. For our traditional female role demanded that we act as compromiser and negotiator. We have held our tongues for the sake of peace, and by denying ourselves expression of our innermost beliefs and cherished principles we have also denied ourselves and our men any possibility of an authentic and growing relationship. This type of pandering to the male ego is finished. Science, as well as our need for greater honesty and integrity in our human relationships, has killed it. But out of the ashes might come, with a strong dollop of luck, the first authentic male-female relationships, relationships freed of false role playing which is the all-pervasive characteristic of most male-female relationships today.

Already our female world has been specifically and fundamentally changed. Use of the birth-control pill, and the biological freedom which it bestows, has shaken traditional social and moral values to their core. We can choose with absolute certitude the number of children we wish to bear. At the same time we have been freed from the cruel stigma that historically attached to barrenness. Barrenness might still prove to be a psychological burden within the privacy of our minds or our marriages, but at least we have been freed from the intrusive pity or scorn of strangers at large, for who is to know whether such barrenness springs from deliberate choice or from a chemical or physiological deficiency, his or hers?

Of equal significance with the biological freedom from the consequences of sexual intercourse has been *the gift of conscience with all its opportunities for true spiritual and intellectual growth*. Our intellectual and spiritual life has always been subservient to our biological nature; it is no accident that in those countries where birth control is outlawed, where the women are sentenced by a male government and a male church to breed year in and year out, that the worst of religious superstitions flourish.

Freedom to accept or reject other relationships, either with persons or with things, is the only environment in which personal growth can take place, but we women have never experienced this freedom. For instance, like most women I have a deep fear of rape. It does not stop me from traveling, from going out at night, from living, but the fear is there and at times—returning to an empty hotel room late at night, for instance—it is very real. I am no different from millions of other women in this respect. Fear of rape

—or more properly fear of evil—is the legacy every woman inherits as a child. Forced penetration by the male penis is the unspoken fear of every parent of every little girl and this fear is forcefully transmitted to us in myriad ways though it is never verbalized or explained. The horror thus takes on another and worse dimension, terror of the unknown.

But now I can move out into the world, involve myself with others, encased in a body I can actually love, a body still vulnerable to rape but free at least of its biological consequences, a body which no longer suffuses my being with the sense of a constant threat. As we are no longer subservient to our biological nature, we can elect to make love or not make love, to have a child or not have a child, to enter into or avoid relationships, our choice being determined not by any impeding fear of bodily consequences but by higher and nobler motives—the good of ourselves or the good of the other or the good of society.

We are expressing this new sense of bodily and spiritual freedom in our fresh perception of our own bodies; they are no longer objects to be corseted and spread with pastes or to be distorted in shape and texture to fulfill a false image. For the first time we are beginning to see our bodies as objects worthy of love and respect in their most natural, spontaneous forms. Younger women are refusing to fetter their breasts with brassieres and butter their faces with makeup, older women are dressing more casually, more comfortably. They are beginning to let their graying hair stay gray, to grow it long, to face the world the way they really are. We are all feeling a new sense of freedom no matter what our age. And, to return to my earlier point, a large part of this sense of body freedom results from an easy and relatively safe form of birth control. Should there be substantial proof that the pill is medically hazardous, it will be only a matter of historical minutes before a substitute is found.

There is one important psychological effect of the pill that I have never heard discussed.

Most women who use the pill know within hours when their period will be due and almost precisely how long it will last and they are gifted thereafter with twenty-eight good days a month. If this benefit appears trivial to the male that is simply because he has never been able to enter into and understand the existential realities of our "monthly" life. This "life" is of more importance to some women than to others. Some women endure miserable periodic cramps. Others of us have never had a cramp in our lives. Whatever our condition, we are all subject to one central reality, and that is we have always been in some form of bondage to this body. What was happening within it at every moment of our adult life was something over which we had no control. There is an edge of defeat in this condition, a vague and misty sense of being caught in a mechanism controlled by time and the vagaries of one's moods, frustrations and passions. For should we catch a common cold, have a sudden fright, or fight with our husband or lover, this could delay the period for a full, agonizing week, long after the cause of the delay had faded from mind.

Men sigh at our dull and trifling periodic complaints, for the cramps don't seem too bad and as for the headaches, everyone gets them. But it is neither the cramps nor headaches that are primarily responsible for the air of petulant malaise that surrounds many females at this time. And note that this petulance is characteristic of the female before the event, seldom during or after it. Why? It is not only because of the building up of hormones. It is because it is at this time that the female whose life-style is one of dependency experiences most intensely her sense of helplessness. What is true of the dependent woman is to a lesser extent true for all of us women. We cannot control an event that is part of our most intimate nature. We cannot control the time, the place or the intensity of that event. And the anger of our frustration and the bile of our passivity are then expressed in petty complaints, such as headaches and cramps, when the true seat of our anger often as not lies in the fact that the affirmation of our womanhood (our dependency) is implicit in that flow of blood, often intense, unexpected, embarrassing and inconvenient.

Now women who take the pill experience a painless, brief and eminently manageable flow. The time can be predicted, the intensity controlled and precautions taken. What this adds up to is that we can plan our time and our lives, our days and our hours, with a full engagement of our human energies unfettered by corrupting uncertainty. The pill (or whatever the form birth control ultimately takes) has given us a gift of time that can be counted in years and a gift of energy that is immeasurable. (How amusing, and revealing of society's hypocrisy, has been the uproar over the safety of the pill while cigarettes, proven beyond any doubt to cause cancer, are peddled freely by the billions.)

Other changes. Scientists can now bank mammalian sperm indefinitely, using it at will to produce viable offspring. They can produce superovulation in the female so that human eggs can be stored for testing and experimentation without destroying their viability. They can regulate the sex of rabbit offspring and if it's rabbits one year it's humans the next. In a few years geneticists will be able to regulate the size of the human brain by prenatal or early postnatal intervention.

A woman already can choose a husband because of characteristics that indicate he would make an ideal living companion but, when picking the father of her child, she will be able in the foreseeable future to draw from a local sperm bank. She will be impregnated if she chooses with the sperm of another man—a musician, scientific genius, athlete, comedian. That women might one day choose one man to live with and the sperm of another to be impregnated with is not so far-fetched if we see how our views in the matter of sexual behavior have changed in the last two decades.

In our world, the world of women, genetic engineering has one central implication: the womb has lost its sovereignty. And it follows that the institution of traditional marriage is not only about to be challenged but faces the threat of obsolescence. I am not speaking here of the future; I am speaking of the now. All around me dozens of young women are living in apparently joyful, and certainly public, cohabitation with their boy friends. To believe that these women are some sort of fringe group—hippies or some type of social drop-outs—is to admit ignorance of what is really happening to the marriage scene today. Why should we marry? they ask. In their eyes the whole world around them is a warning not to marry. They quote their friends who have married, had babies, and have shriveled up and died inside. All that they say expresses their perception of traditional marriage as an out-and-out form of oppression, which it most certainly is. They don't want to go into their graves waiting for something to happen to them, as their mothers did. And that is what traditional marriage means for them—the end of growth, the end of exploration, investigation, of new experiences and new self-knowledge. The instant you become "a wife" you are no longer "a woman." "Give me just one good reason," they ask, "why I should want to be part of an institution that diminishes life for both partners?"

Within marriage there is increasing resistance to the notion that the woman who devotes her life entirely to house and family is automatically a better wife and mother than she who goes out to work. Hundreds of thousands of married women are joining the labor force annually. They say they need the money, or are sick and tired of housework, or fed up with feeling guilty over every penny spent. Whatever they say, it adds up to one thing—the desire to become "somebody." Not an important person, just a full-fledged member of the human race who no longer wishes to spend her days and years in suburban solitary confinement.

This breaking out of the doll's house has as much meaning for the male as for the female. It is the beginning of *his* liberation. It means the demise of his mandatory role of breadwinner. If he chooses to play this role, it will be a choice made in the face of other alternatives. Among such possible alternatives: husband and wife working part-time only so that they both can spend more time with the children; the husband staying at home and running the house while the woman takes outside employment; either or both working, but for a limited salary, in a job that is socially constructive and personally enriching. What we are beginning to understand for the first time is that many traditional marriages are worse than a form of legalized prostitution. The prostitute and her client at least are honest about what they seek from each other.

Scientific changes are not only preparing us to break out of our traditional roles; they are systematically destroying many of our sex role images. For the first time it is becoming possible that we might experience what men have always taken for granted—the choice of a life-long occupation or occupations.

It is a fact that this choice of the male is often as not illusory. With all the dreams men have, the majority end up planting corn, digging in a mine, driving a truck or shuffling paper, stuck in their places like flies in jam. Yet there is a profound difference between a man's lot and a woman's. If he does not actually have a choice of occupation and a control over the expenditure of his years, he—at least for his growing years—*thinks* he has and as a child this invests his games and all his contacts with the world with an exploratory element. He grows up with a *sense* of freedom and a *chance* of having freedom of choice. Nobody has told him time and time again that he must dig ditches all his life, or bake bread, or teach school. His maleness released the restraints on his perceived future, whereas our femaleness automatically locks us into the dimensions of the house. Because we have not experienced this sense of free destiny, most of us lack the critical growth of imagination that should have accompanied it.

One critical sex role that has been destroyed is that of the male as my protector. The last twenty-five years of history have proven this male role to be nothing but a myth. Nobody knows better than the Japanese woman the impotence of the male compared to the bomb. (But a Japanese wife is still expected to call her husband "Shunjin," meaning "Master.") Jewish women, who watched every member of the family destroyed by the Nazis, know the impotence of the male. (Yet in his matutinal prayers the orthodox Jew still offers thanks to God that he was not born a woman.) What Biafran, Vietnamese, South African woman —or what American woman—would be so naïve as to depend on a man for protection against famine or nuclear annihilation? There appears to be no American male alive today who can adequately protect his women against rape on city streets in broad daylight.

This concept of the male as the protector of the female has played a primary role in all male-female relationships for centuries. Its loss will precipitate a radical restructuring of relationships between the sexes, for the concept of the "weak" female leaps up as a lie. As it turns out we are all as weak, as helpless and as trapped. Yet the men are still asking: "What do these women want anyway, to grow beards?" And they are asking it totally unaware that the hostile categorization of "these women" and the stale quip about beards express a great deal of what women's liberation is all about. But these are all peripheral issues.

*At the heart of the female revolution there is an anguish that proceeds from a harsh reality—large numbers of chil-*

*dren are no longer needed to perpetuate the species. Because woman has gained no corporate strength in modern society she faces the fundamental problem of her very existence.* By corporate strength I mean the power to introduce change and the muscle to effect it.

For centuries, we have done our own thing and we have done it with a lot of inner life, with hate, love, joy, frustration, anger and pride. No matter how we did it, there was no contradiction between our act and society's needs.

But today women must ask themselves, who and what am I? Who am I to become, whom shall I love and for whom or what shall I work and struggle if children are no longer needed?

What am I to do with my life?

# CHAPTER

# II

During the last decade science has made a discovery whose implications in the realm of women seem largely to have been ignored. And that is this: *Every cell in the body of the female is chemically different from every cell in the body of the male. The male and the female are materially different down to the very marrow of their bones.*

We women now *know* we are not "deficient males" as Aristotle and Thomas Aquinas, and later Freud, insisted. We are not an imitation of the male or even a warped facsimile. We are women, different and equal. Our intellects, our perceptions, feelings, relationships are uniquely ours and in every sense are as legitimate, worthy, valid as the male's.

In the essence of my being there is an element that is sexual. This sexuality is a female sexuality and it is an integral component of my entire being. Stated another way, there are forty-six chromosomes in each cell of my female body and one of those chromosomes in each cell is always an X. In the body of the male, one of the chromosomes in each cell is always a Y. In the simplest terms this means that the body and brain of the female differ materially from every cell in the body and brain of the male—that there is a sexuality in the essence of each person's being and this essence of being cannot be changed. With every denial or distortion of this essence through the aping of the other sex there is a proportionate loss of authenticity and, as a result, a loss of inner strength and integrity.

As we absorb all the implications of being "different but equal" we will drop a painful burden of centuries. The burden I refer to is the female imperative to compare, consciously or unconsciously, every feeling and reaction with those to be expected of the mythical male who monitors all that dwells within the female skull. We will for the first time understand that male feelings, reactions, perceptions have no greater validity or authority than ours. We will cease to give a damn what the male thinks of our laughter or tears, of our method of operation, passion or passivity, nor will we react to his petrified concepts of what areas are suitable for our intellectual and social concerns. We will know that we are not male and can never be male, that he is not female and can never be female, and this knowledge will bring us freedom. In the past, our difference from the male has been a crippling, intimidating factor. In the future this difference will be the catalyst of our growth.

Now that science has proven a basic chemical difference, it becomes clear why the feminist movements of the past have failed. They were doomed from the start for they were based on the fiction that the difference between male and female was a difference of accident and not substance, of matter not form—a difference of such externals as geni-

talia, muscular development and education. Feminists of
the past believed that given the chance woman could become *like* man. They saw man as an oppressor, as it happened, but what they clearly understood was the context in
which man operated, and in that context it was necessary to
be male to be free. One can only hazard a guess at the
courage it took for some of these early female fighters to
take on the male world as they did; even today, when the
sluggish-minded male takes it for granted that women are
equal like a good maid is equal, the feminist must pay
harsh dues in terms of the malice and derision to be borne.

The feminist movements were doomed for a second, if
parallel, reason. They were doomed because in an attempt
to break into the male-institutionalized world they repressed their own authentic and uniquely generic impulses.
Woman knows that men are violent yet call it strength, are
aggressive yet call it courage, are cruel yet call it justice,
are unjust yet call it intelligence. We know that and yet
today, as in the past, many of us still struggle to ape men.
Why? Because the burden of our "difference" from the male
has been made intolerable by him. If we are just we are dis-
regarded, if compassionate we are ignored. Men laugh at
our conscience, deride our strength, belittle our courage. It
is true that the just and compassionate person of either sex
will receive harsh treatment from the male-institutionalized
world. But for us women the snubbing is less tolerable because we are more impotent socially. Further, it exacer-
bates our sense of being trapped within a femaleness that
automatically shuts off the world of the possible.

A measure of the possible changes in attitude that the
discovery of the chromosomal difference might bring has

been provided by several United States law courts in the handling of criminal cases. Geneticists have found that, while the normal male has forty-six chromosomes, some men have forty-seven, that is, an extra Y. Some geneticists claim that this XYY syndrome produces a male who is tall, given to acne, aggressive and antisocial.

In New York on January 21, 1969, Sean Farley, an accused rape-slayer, pleaded not guilty by reason of insanity. His attorney claimed Farley was not responsible for his acts as he possessed an extra male chromosome. On the same day in Los Angeles, Raymond Tanner, charged with assaulting a woman, changed his plea from guilty to not guilty following medical tests which indicated he possessed a second male Y chromosome.

Implicit in these defenses is the fact that possession of the XY chromosome appears to be the norm in determining legal and civil responsibility, as well as one's capacity to adhere to the norms of societal behavior and goals. But what about the other half of mankind? What about us—the other 100 million residents of North America, not to mention the women of the rest of the world, who do not have the "norm" of the XY chromosome but have a chromosomal differentiate that is as far removed from the XY norm as is the criminal XYY component? Every institution which dominates our lives—state, church, marriage, education, the military, etc.—was created by those who possessed the XY chromosome, the males. The theoretical question arises —are we women bound to accept and adhere to goals, morals, laws and a world view that have been created, motivated and sustained solely by possessors of the XY chromosome?

What will happen when the mass of women realize the validity of their own perceptions and world view? It might
well be that nothing will happen, that female perceptions
and world views will coincide with those of the male. But it
is just possible that, freed from a false theory of themselves,
women will take their own stance, will say: "War is insanity
and I will no longer support it in any way whatsoever." Or:
"These laws are discriminatory and I will go to prison before I obey them." Or: "I am taking my child out of the
school system because it is destructive both to her creativity
and humanity." Or: "I will buy no more products from any
exploited area of the world, no detergent that will pollute
the waters, no automobile that will foul the air."

If it is the female's capacity to act authentically and
spontaneously as a female, and not as an imitation male,
that will ultimately give us corporate strength, we must ask:
What is authentic woman? What are masculine and feminine
characteristics? Have men and women merely learned
under social pressure to take on certain behavior patterns
that society has defined as appropriate? Or are the different
behavior patterns the result of the basic chromosomal difference?

It is a fact that every society differentiates between the
roles prescribed for each sex. It is just as true that these
roles vary from culture to culture. The thesis that sex differences are largely culturally determined was expounded
by anthropologist Margaret Mead in her study of the Arapesh, Tchambuli and the Mundugumor tribes of New
Guinea. The Arapesh considered that a gentle temperament
—what this society would label as "feminine" behavior
patterns—was ideal for both sexes. The Mundugumor so-

ciety was characterized by hostile, aggressive, violent and insensitive behavior by both male and female members— all characteristics that our North American society would consider "masculine." The Tchambuli tribe held that women should be practical, domineering and aggressive especially in sexual matters, while the ideal male behavior pattern was to be sensitive, artistic, well groomed, emotional and dependent.

A number of anthropologists and social scientists have provided further data in support of Dr. Mead's thesis that sex roles result from social learning rather than from biologically inherited tendencies. Anthropologist Ethel Albert, author of *Women of Tropical Africa* (1963) and *People of Rimrock: A Study of Values in Five Cultures* (1966), noted that it was the women of the Central African tribes who did the hard, manual labor; the men believed they were not suited by nature to engage in sustained toil. Albert also notes the vast difference in "appropriate" sex behavior, the women of some African and American Indian societies being highly sexually aggressive compared to the norm of passive and compliant males. In *The Silent Language* (1959), Edward Hall points out that the emotional roles of the Iranian male and female are the opposite of the sex roles played out in Western society. The women are expected to be logical and practical, the men to show their feelings, be sensitive, intuitive and perceptive.

Anthropological studies abound with evidence of this sort. Yet it appears to me that *there is a critical difference between male and female* that is outside and apart from any social conditioning and learned response.

This critical difference is the sexuality as determined by the chromosomes—sexuality not as a genetic or genital difference, but as an integral part of a person's totality. Within this context, male and female are eternally and irreconcilably different. It is impossible to define or categorize this element of sexuality. We cannot say that male sexuality is this or that female sexuality is that. We have tried to do this over the centuries by denying the vast range of temperamental differences between one male and another and one female and another. For instance, we categorize the gentle boy as a "sissy" and the aggressive little girl as a "tomboy." Sexuality is the most deeply personal and unique element in the makeup of any human being. The man or the woman who is successful in integrating sexuality with the rest of his or her emotions, beliefs, life-style, ideals, and realities, such as age, is a fully realized human being. He or she who fails to do so is doomed to a lifelong struggle. Although we cannot put our finger on this precise element of sexuality, we recognize its all-pervasive quality when we say that such-and-such a man or woman is "a fabulous person" or "terribly attractive" or "just so sexy." Often such a person will be physically plain or advanced in age; what we recognize and are drawn to is a certain vitality, a fierce life force, a force that attracts and draws the opposite sex. For within each individual's sexuality there is an incompleteness that depends on the opposite sex for completeness. The two sexes are complementary to each other. This positive-negative pull seems to be a natural law that is apart from any social conditioning. The male needs a female for the fulfillment of his totality as a human being; the female needs a male for the same reason. This need has been determined by the individual's chromosomes. The coming together of the sexes is the basic dynamic of all nature.

I believe that this sexuality—as part of a human being's totality—is, with one minor exception, the sole difference between male and female. The minor exception is this: woman spends nine months carrying a child within her and man does not. This biological conditioning has evolved within her a characteristic that is not shared by the average male. The nurturing of the very small elements of life has given her an ability to handle detail and a capacity for great patience. Because of her biological conditioning, it appears to be more woman's nature than man's to nurture small things; in this, and in this alone, she differs from man. Later, we will see how important this secondary female characteristic might become in a world that has such a need for the nurturing and nourishing to maturity of all kinds of people and things. We will also see how, without a proper orientation, this capacity for detail becomes a pettiness.

As for the rest of the alleged male and female "inborn" differences, we are what society over hundreds of thousands of years has conditioned us into being. This is as true for the male as the female. Is that poor eviscerated bull pushing a shopping cart through the supermarket really a *man?* He, too, has been so programmed to act out the image of male imposed upon him that separating the preconditioned or "natural" tendencies from today's learned behavior presents an impossible task. To extricate preconditioned, "natural" woman from the man-made rules of centuries is even more complex.

It has been man, not woman, who has written all the romantic literature and poetry in all civilizations. Through these constructs, man has developed a clear idea of what *he* considers desirable and attractive, hence necessary, in a woman. Through these constructs he has pronounced on what is "feminine" and what is "unfeminine," on what traits in women are worthy of male approval and support and what traits should be rigorously condemned. Analyze the characteristics the male lauds most highly as suitable for the female over the centuries and they are strikingly comparable to the willing servant's—obedience, humility, modesty, simplicity, chastity, cheerfulness, domestic skills. Rarely has the male praised female courage, honesty, spirit, independence, determination and intelligence. These characteristics are "masculine," hence undesirable in a woman. Who has heard of an intelligent and independent woman making a good servant?

Man did not stop at selecting "characteristics" suitable for his purposes. He went to the extreme of dictating the proper and acceptable female reactions to such a conglomerate of events as birth, child-rearing, love, marriage, sex, education, old age, dress, work and death. Man through literature, and later through his institutions, laid out all the rules of all the games, spelling out quite precisely what woman must be and what she could or could not do to meet his approval. If woman failed to comply she quite frequently was subjected to penalties characterized by a diabolical cruelty, such as drowning women who aborted an unwanted pregnancy.

In terms of power, it paid man to limit the image of the desirable female within a biological context and, conversely, to damn as "unnatural" or "unfeminine" any qualities, such as ambition, that would free her from this context. Woman, lacking contraception and hence any control over her physical existence, proved an easy object for domination. The result of this process is that many a modern woman has a deep conviction of her "natural" inferiority, a fear of the outside world, and a sense of overwhelming hopelessness in trying to deal with it.

These feelings of inferiority are so ingrained that the strongest anti-female prejudice often exists among other women. Women *do* believe their own sex to be inferior. In Gordon W. Allport's *The Nature of Prejudice* he claims that antifeminism is not so much an active belief as a deep bias that *distorts all perception and experience,* including the alleged "evidence" on which the prejudiced person bases his or her beliefs. Important though *The Nature of Prejudice* is, it merely confirms what the career woman already knows—that distortion of her actions and her image is part of the dues she must pay as the scapegoat of so much female frustration.

One of the most fascinating studies on female prejudice towards other women was conducted by Dr. Philip Goldberg, associate professor of psychology at Connecticut College.* In this study, Dr. Goldberg took six articles and combined them into two identical booklets. The same article bore a male author's name in one booklet, a female author's name in the other. (If in Set One the first article bore the name John T. McKay, in Set Two the same article would appear under the name Joan T. McKay.) Each

* "Women Are Inferior—So Women Think," *Trans-action,* Washington University, St. Louis, Missouri, 1968.

booklet contained three articles by "men" and three articles by "women."

In the instructions given the 140 college girl subjects, no mention was made of the authors' sexes. That information was presented without comment and just as an incidental part of a much larger project—or so the subjects thought. The girls were merely told that there were six articles, written by six different authors in six different professional fields. They were asked to make critical evaluations, these to be based on value, persuasiveness and profundity—and to rate the authors for writing style, professional competence, professional status and ability to sway the reader. The conclusion:

> Though the articles themselves were exactly the same, the girls felt that those written by the John T. McKays were definitely more impressive, and reflected more glory on their authors, than did the mediocre offerings of the Joan T. McKays.
>
> Perhaps because the world has accepted female authors for a long time, the girls were willing to concede that the female professionals' writing styles were not *far* inferior to those of the men. But such a concession to female competence was rare indeed.

Dr. Goldberg concludes that "whatever lip services these girls pay to modern ideas of equality between men and women, their beliefs are staunchly traditional. Their real coach in the battle of the sexes is not Simone de Beauvoir or Betty Friedan. Their coach is Aristotle."

CHAPTER

# III

As I enjoy working in the man's world, and consider house-work the perfect drag, some men undoubtedly think of me as a hard-nosed bitch. Whether I am or not, I have the Greeks to thank for this. For the role that they determined for women 2,500 years ago is my legacy as a woman today. They piped the tune and with few exceptions every writer and philosopher since has danced to it.

The importance of the role played by the Greeks in sub-jugating women cannot be overestimated. For until the Greeks seized upon language as a conceptual tool nothing approaching a philosophy had been put into writing. Until their time, written language was confined to simple ac-counting and mathematics, or the depiction of wars, royal festivities and the like, such as in the cuneiforms of Baby-lon or the hieroglyphics of Egypt. It was the Greeks who formulated and then recorded a rationalized schema that justified the institutions already in existence, including slav-ery and the inferiority of women.

It was the Greeks who told me how to act in marriage, feel towards war, relate to my children, act in pregnancy, how to make love, live, die and breathe. It was the Greeks who said I was "a deficient male," who called the religious woman "a hag" and the passionate woman "a harlot." It was the Greeks who said that the courage of a man is shown in commanding and in a woman in obeying. They did their work so well that literature through the ages became the perfect and unquestioned medium through which man could express with impunity his loathing of, and superiority over, the female. Remember that not only has the bulk of the world's literature been the creation of men, but that the technical production and control of its distribution lies to this day almost exclusively in male hands.

We have never poured out *our* hearts. We have never said what *we* think is desirable in a man. We have never described the qualities we love and cherish, nor what we consider to be a beautiful male, nor how we want males to act or not to act. Men did this for us. They not only told us what they considered desirable in a female; they also dictated to us what we should consider attractive in the male.

Aeschylus' play, *Seven Against Thebes,* circa 500 B.C., contains one of the first written references to woman:

> Oh, you intolerable pack, you hags!
> Will't help the city, think you? Will't inspire
> A bold assurance in the beleaguered troops
> To cast you down before those antique shapes
> Our holy guardians, there to rave and howl—
> Objects, disgusted, decency abhors!
> Good times, bad times, may I never house
> With womankind!

The use of literature as a misogynist tool was on its way. In *Andromache,* Euripides counsels me in the year 450 B.C. as to the correct marital attitudes of the virtuous woman. "Take heed," says Andromache, "for a woman bestowed upon a worthless husband must be with him content." She then speaks of her life with Hector:

> For thy sake would I brook a rival . . . and oft in days gone by I held thy bastard babes to my own breast to spare thee any cause of grief. By this course I bound my husband to me by virtue's chains.

Later, Hermione soliloquizes:

> Oh never, never should men of sense who have wives allow women-folk to visit them in their homes, for they teach them mischief; one to gain some private ends, helps corrupt their honor: another, having made a slip herself, wants a companion in misfortune, while many are wantons —and hence it is men's houses are tainted.

I am not about to teach anyone mischief, corrupt another's honor, become a wanton—but Euripides said I was. Nor am I about to seduce, rob, stab and blind, as Polymnestor, another Euripidean character, suggests in *Hecuba.* Sighing, he gently shafts us:

> If any of the men of former times have spoken ill of women, if any doth so now, or shall do so hereafter, all this in one short sentence shall I say: neither land or sea produces a race so pestilent, as whosoever have had to do with them knows full well.

Later, in Euripides' *The Phoenician Maidens* I am told how all my sisters love to gossip and "seem to take a pleasure in saying everything bad of one another. When Lysistrata in the play of the same name grieves for the sake of womankind "because the men account us to be sly, shifty rogues," Euripides had Calonice reply, "And so, by Zeus, we are." And so I become with Lysistrata a shy and shifty rogue in male eyes.

Plato indicates he was not quite sure what we are. In his *Republic* he advocates our equality in the new society, even to being trained in arms and warfare. But in his *Dialogues,* the Athenian stranger warns:

> . . . and just that part of human nature which is prone to secrecy and stealth on account of their weakness—I mean the female sex—has been left without regulators . . . in proportion as women's nature is inferior to men in capacity of virtue . . . women are accustomed to creep into dark places and when dragged out into the light they will exert their utmost powers of resistance.

If we inserted the word "black" for "women" in these plays they would be banned today throughout the United States just like *Little Black Sambo.* All these quotations are typical of the first literary references to women. In the *History of Animals,* Aristotle speaks with the authority of science necessary to preserve these views for centuries.

> A boy is like a woman in form, and the woman is, as it were, an impotent male, for it is through a certain incapacity that the female is female, being incapable of concocting the nutrient in its last stages into semen.

And so I became fixed in male eyes as some kind of half-formed, half-baked human, a creation that results from weakness and incapacity. This theme of the female as a sort of runt in the family litter undoubtedly assured popular success even in those times. It not only denigrated the female but blew up the "capacity" (the penis) of the male until, in the *History of Animals,* the unstated theme of the male as stallion, free, strong and virile, is covertly expressed in this manner:

> ... of all animals, the woman and the mare are most inclined to receive the commerce of the male during pregnancy.

Skillfully, Aristotle makes deficiency in any form synonymous with female. Even those who cannot conceive without medical help are "as a general rule apt to bear female children rather than male." And the bearing of one of these runted female offspring naturally extracts a punishment.

> As a general rule, women who are pregnant with a male child escape (bad health) comparatively easily and retain a comparatively healthy look, but it is otherwise with those whose infants are female, for these latter look as a rule paler and suffer more pain and in many cases are subject to swellings of the legs and eruptions of the body.

What does this mean? Simply, to carry a female child within one's body is similar to harboring a contagion, a sickness, a deficient and unhealthy form of life that in the very nature of things spreads a score of well-deserved afflictions throughout the host body.

Women in pregnancy are a prey to all sorts of longings and with the mothers of female infants the longings are more acute and they are less contented when they have got what they desired.

Part of the "fault" in bearing a female, Aristotle concedes, lies with the male, "for when the spermatic fluid is thin it is infertile: when granular it is fertile and likely to produce male children, but when thin and unclotted it is apt to produce female offspring."

With my female body consigned to limbo, Aristotle then started in on my female mind. This is how he propagandized in his *Rhetoric,* Book I:

One action is nobler than another if it is that of a naturally finer being: thus a man's will be nobler than a woman.

Clearly, moral virtue belonged to all:

. . . but the temperance of a man or a woman, or the courage and justice of a man and a woman are not, as Socrates maintained, the same: the courage of a man is shown in commanding, the woman in obeying. For as Sophocles said, "Silence is a woman's glory but this is not equally the glory of man."

Indeed, in *On the Generation of Animals* Aristotle teaches that it is imperative men understand that I and all other women "are weaker and colder by nature" than men. That is because I, being a woman, am "naturally deficient."

We must look upon the female character as being a sort of natural deficiency. Accordingly, while it is within the mother it develops slowly because of its coldness: but after birth it quickly arrives at maturity and old age on account of its weakness, for all inferior things come sooner to their perfection or end.

Now I am not a hag, a member of a pestilential race, nor am I destructive, a lover of gossip, sly and shifty, prone to stealth, inferior in virtue, a deficient being, an impotent male. But the Greeks said I am; they said all women are and to this day their dehumanizing concepts flourish. They said, too, that if I become an active participant in love-making I become a harlot. Lucretius in *The Nature of Things,* Book IV, verbalizes the male fear of female sexuality that is just as real today.

Nor have wives the least use of effeminate notions: a woman hinders and stands in the way of her own conceiving when thus she acts, for she drives the furrow out of the direct course and path of the share and turns away from the proper spot the stroke of the seed. And thus for their own end harlots are wont to move, in order not to conceive and lie in child-bed frequently, and at the same time to render Venus more attractive to men. This our wives have surely no need of.

If we go from Lucretius, who died about 55 B.C. (from an overdose of a love potion), to Augustine 400 years later we find the same sick fear of our female sexuality: it ensnares the male with its offer of pleasure but taints his soul with shame.

Lust requires for its consummation darkness and secrecy, and this not only when unlawful intercourse is desired but even such fornication as the earthly city has legalized.

And while lust found it easy to remove the prohibitions
of law, shamelessness found it impossible to lay aside the
veil of retirement. For even shameless men call this
shameful; and though they love the pleasure, dare not display it. . . . The right action dreads to be seen. And why
so, if not because that which is by nature fitting and decent
is so done as to be accomplished with a shame-begetting
penalty of sin? (*The City of God,* Book 14)

It would be difficult to exaggerate the harm done to male
and female relationships to this day by such outpourings.
Yet how could the Greeks have hammered their concepts
so deep into man, even modern man living in a world trans-
formed by science and technology, unless they contained an
inherent truth?

The answer is simply that while man's technological capacity has developed his emotions are still locked into the
thirteenth century.

In thirteenth-century Europe, the Church was the sole
repository of knowledge. All universities were under its
domination; all known science and literature were guarded
and disseminated through its portals. The church was, as it
is today, a male-dominated institution with its views of
women culled from the Bible (which was written at much
the same historic moment that the Greeks were formalizing
their philosophy) and reinforced by the teachings of the Pa-
tristic Fathers. (Mary Day in *The Church and the Second
Sex* has treated this theme brilliantly.)

All the ingredients that might ensure the perpetuation of
women's subservience were present, except one, and that
missing ingredient was a forceful conceptual tool. Aristotle,
through the master theologian, Thomas Aquinas, provided

it. For hundreds of years prior to this time the Eastern sector of Europe had been sealed off by the Moslems to all but itinerant travelers and traders. Then, via the Moors of Spain, Aristotle was brought back to Europe and his works quickly fell into the hands of Aquinas. It was only a matter of time before Aquinas took over for himself the Aristotelian notion of "fixed" natures—that women played only a minor role in procreation. They supplied merely the *matter,* while the superior being, the male, supplied the *form* or soul.

> As regards the particular nature, woman is defective and misbegotten, for the active force in the male seed tends to the production of a perfect likeness in the masculine sex, while the production of woman comes from defect in the active force or from some external change, such as that of a south wind, which is moist, as the philosopher (Aristotle) observes. (*Summa Theologica,* First Part, Q 92, Arts 2)

Here was the vindication that a celibate clergy had been waiting for. And so in this manner the Church provided the bridge upon which the concepts of the Greeks crossed from the first to the twentieth century.

It was at this point, as Mary Daly indicates, that as the subjugation of woman crystallized in practice, devotion to the Virgin Mary began to flourish. For Mary is innocence, passivity, matter and object, the very antithesis of a creative, exploratory and authentic human being. One notes that in those countries where Mary is most adulated, the status of women is lowest. The masses of female poor are little better than biological beasts of burden, prostitution flourishes and the mistress system is an integral part of any marital relationship. Consider in psychological terms the implications of the image of the woman who is a mother while yet a virgin. Mary is everything no other woman can be—female but an instrument of God and not the devil, a mother but untainted by the sensuality of sex. Shrouded in mystery, her image epitomizes the destiny that man in those times was consolidating for all of womankind. Slowly the image of woman, as conjured up by man, was being consolidated. Mary R. Beard in *Woman as Force in History* says:

> In the numberless mediaeval records which indicate men's ideas of women, all kinds of formulas appear again and again. Thus, women are cleaner and better than men; by their virtues they lift men above masculine grossness, vulgarity and brutality; they bear the heavy burden of civilizing men. Again, women are inherently sinful and wicked, the originators and abettors of evil; they are forward in their insolence; they have commerce with the devil, resort to magic, and in general must be subdued to the ordinances of the priests if not to other men; they should be humble and obedient to their husbands; and it is not meet for them to invade man's domain.

So the written word became man's chief weapon in molding an image of woman most suitable for his domination and usage. While on one hand she was conjured up as a creature of delicacy and virtue, on the other care was taken to keep her ultimate status questionable, if not degraded. Rabelais, as one example, depicts the female as a tonic; her relationship to the male is that of an object which irrigates the colon.

But Panurge replies truly, he found a great deal of good in the counsel of woman, chiefly in that of the old wives, for every time I consult with them I readily get a stool or two extraordinary to the great solace of my bum-gut passage. (*Pantagruel*)

Montaigne expounded on the nature of woman with somewhat more delicacy but the sum total of his image of woman is no more enlightened than Rabelais'. They were people of "irregular appetite and depraved tastes." And as for women who were not physically beautiful but had the audacity to believe that despite this they were still worthy of male love and respect, why, these stupid creatures were like the Brahmin virgins who

> having no other beauty to recommend them—the people being assembled by the common crier to that effect—come out into the market place to expose their matrimonial parts to public view, to see if these at least won't get them a husband. (Essay III)

It is ironic that the same man writes of his soul's longing for a marriage that would be "a free and voluntary familiarity where not only the souls might have this fruition but where the bodies might join in the alliance." Ironic, because by Montaigne's own admission his views on woman "coincide" with the "common consent of the ancient schools." What is probably closer to the truth is that Montaigne was brainwashed in his youth by the Greeks and later lacked the intellectual ballsiness necessary to liberate the women in his own personal life. And so he cheated

himself of the psychological and physical intimacy which
he craved, just as men go on cheating themselves today, unable to grasp the fundamental fact that oppression automatically precludes love.

With Chaucer, Shakespeare and Cervantes there is consid-
erable cracking in the now-hardened construct of the
female as inferior; woman is shown as tough, ambitious,
lustful, shrewd and often bawdy. But to Milton we were
serpents:

> Out of my sight thou serpent, that name
> Best befits thee with him leaguered, thyself
>     as false
> And hateful; nothing wants but that thy shape,
> Like his, and colour Serpentine may show
> Thy inward fraud, to warn all Creatures
>     from thee
> Henceforth; least that too heavenly form,
>     pretended
> To hellish falsehood, snare them. But for thee
> I had persisted happie. . . . (*Paradise Lost*)

Quite a splendid example of psychiatrist Eric Berne's *IIWFY*
game—"If It Weren't For You."

By the early 1700s Jonathan Swift was striking out for
the education of girls, deriding his country where one half
of the population "is good for nothing but bringing children
into the world, and to trust the care of their children to
such useless animals was yet a greater instance of brutal-
ity." But by this time the idea of woman as "useless animals" was flourishing, if invisible. The total social unconscious was pervaded with it. Squire Western in Henry

Fielding's *Tom Jones* spoke for the males of the Western world when he said we women "should come in with the first dish and go out after the first glass." And as for us having ideas and promulgating them, why, Dr. Samuel Johnson handled that question by comparing women to dogs walking on hind legs:

> I told him that I had been that morning at a meeting of people called Quakers, where I heard a woman preach. Johnson: "Sir, a woman's preaching is like a dog's walking on his hinder legs. It is not done well; but you are surprised to find it done at all." (*Life of Samuel Johnson*, James Boswell)

At the same time Hegel, whose thought is still a critical component in intellectual life today, was saying this about us:

> Women are capable of education, but they are not made for activities which demand a universal faculty such as the more advanced sciences, philosophy, and certain forms of artistic production. Women may have happy ideas, tastes and elegance but they cannot attain to the ideal. The difference between men and women is like that between animals and plants. Men correspond to animals while women correspond to plants because their development is more placid and the principle that underlies it is the rather vague unity of feeling. When women hold the helm of government the state is at once in jeopardy, because women regulate their actions not by the demands of universality but by arbitrary inclinations and opinions. Women are educated—who knows why?—as it were by breathing in ideas, by living rather than by acquiring knowledge. The status of manhood, on the other hand, is attained only by

the stress of thought and much technical exertion. (George Wilhelm Friedrich Hegel, *Philosophy of Right,* Para. 166)

The actual gist of this quotation, written by Hegel in Germany in the early nineteenth century, could have come right from the pen of Norman Mailer, New York, 1970.

John Stuart Mill did not confuse misogynism for intellectualism. In his essay *On Liberty* written in 1859 he launched an assault on the male world for teaching woman "that marriage is the one thing needful." Indeed, if there was one relationship that was destructive to woman it was the "despotic power of husbands over wives."

> A person should be free to do as he likes in his own concerns but he ought not to be free as he likes in acting for another under the pretext that the affairs of the other are his own affairs. The state, while it respects the liberty of each in what specially regards himself, is bound to maintain a vigilant control over his exercise of any power which it allows him to possess over others. This obligation is almost entirely disregarded in the case of family relations, a case which, in its direct influence on human happiness, is more important than all others taken together. The almost despotic power of husbands over wives need not be enlarged here for nothing more is needed for the complete removal of the evil than that wives should have the same rights. . . .

Because of the industrial revolution the world was rapidly changing. The family was breaking down. Thousands of farmers, farm laborers and their families were leaving the land and going into the city. There were new sights to be seen, new things to do, new skills to learn, new trades to develop, new thoughts to ponder on. The time was ripe for a total revision of the image and the role of woman. At this historic moment the concept of us as "deficient males" could have been destroyed. But it was too late.

Three years before Mill wrote his essay *On Liberty* Sigmund Freud was born. A great new science was in the offing—or so it seemed. But, once again, the authority that this science drew to it was to be used not as an instrument to liberate half the human race, the female half, but was to become the most powerful intellectual component in modern thought in keeping woman subservient.

Freud was to take man into the dark spots of his soul, on trips in and out of his conscious and unconscious. The nature of all these trips was exploratory; the ends were left wide open. But for woman, the journeys were destined to take a prearranged route. For before the concepts of psychiatry were born within the vault of Freud's brain, his perception of us as inferior beings was as embedded as an inoperable tumor.

# CHAPTER

# IV

My feelings about Freud are admittedly personal and I offer them as such. Once I went to a psychiatrist, went in desperation, went in an openness and sincerity that was total, went when the financial cost was almost worse than the disease, only to find the stale breath of Freud's misogyny meeting me at every turn. I mention this because it is a common experience of women who seek psychiatric help; they seek it unaware that as they move into that office they are being perceived through a set of concepts that are as outmoded and irrelevant as Aristotelian science. They are unaware that they are entering into a classic psychological operation, a form of guerrilla warfare in which they will be robbed of their courage to be themselves, because Freud defeats his female patients coming or going. He defeats them merely by defining his own terms: what is wrong with woman is that she lacks a penis—and his entire attitude towards women and their treatment rests on this premise.

Should she protest, the protest constitutes proof of his argument.

One instance from my own experience: I had been producing a brief film segment for RKO in New York and raced late into the psychiatrist's office in my work clothes —beige slacks and beige sweater. Said the professional wise man, "Your masculinity is showing today." I replied, "Not at all. These clothes are the most suitable ones in my limited wardrobe for the weather and the outdoor work that I am doing." At this he giggled and, leaning back in his chair, pronounced judgment: "Me thinketh she doth protest too much." He could have told me he was God and had created me with all my memories ten minutes earlier and there would have been no way to disprove him. (It was left to me to sublimate the fact that he wore elevator shoes.)

Now on the brink of middle age, I face the painful fact of years wasted running in the shadow of man, *acting* as if the mere fact of his maleness invested in him superior wisdom. I did not believe this—there was too much evidence to the contrary—but I *acted* as if it were so, lacking the courage and strength to be myself.

The vibrations of Freud's genius could have changed the world: we can only speculate as to what the world might have been had women been freed these last 100 years. He could have destroyed the myths of the feminine mystique as incisively as he destroyed notions of absolute good and evil. He had the genius, the power and the international reputation of having sprung the female mind out of its constructed cage as no other force could have sprung it. Instead, to this day almost all women who undergo psychiatric care are

subtly but persistently channeled back into domesticity, despite the fact that it might well have been the abberation of
living within four walls that sent them to the psychiatrist in
the first place. I am like an unknown number of other
women: what should have been my most creative years
have been spent in combat with myself because my basic
drives were neither towards domesticity or subservience. I
was aware even as a child that while the domestication of
the female was her alleged "glory," KP in the Army was
used as a punishment.

To say that Freud was a victim of his culture and times
is to beg the issue—the misogynistic philosophy at the root
of all his thinking is still a critical component of all intellectual functions today. Freud spared no effort in probing the
shadow side of man and releasing him from the guilts and
fears of centuries. He did this by categorically rejecting
some of the most basic traditional concepts of man. When he
turned to examine woman, it was with a mind hermetically
sealed by the Greek concepts. How can that be explained?
Philip Rief in *Freud: The Mind of a Moralist* says that a
denial of the Freudian psychology of women cannot depend on historical reduction of Freud's own psychology:

It is not enough to say that Freud himself reproduced the
"masculine" protest characteristic of his time and place.
His misogyny, like that of his predecessors, is more than
prejudice: it has a vital intellectual function in his system.
In the nineteenth century, strong links, the forging of
which have not yet been closely studied, existed between
irrational philosophy and misogyny. Freud's view echoes
those of Schopenhauer (in the essay "On Woman") and
Nietzsche. And just as sympathetic expositors of Schopen-

hauer and Nietzsche want to dismiss these philosophers' views on women as idiosyncratic . . . so the neo-Freudians (led by eminent women analysts like Karen Horney) would like to omit that part of Freud's work as mere culture-prejudice maintaining that much of the remaining doctrine can be realigned without damage. But actually the pejorative image of woman serves as a measure of the general critical component of western philosophies . . . a fact the significance of which has not yet been properly assessed.

Rief is suggesting that perhaps the basic philosophic circuit on which our lives are jerked along is more verbal than real and if anybody opened up that particular Pandora's box of the female construct, traditional philosophy might appear as half-mad. And, in particular, if the role played by Freud in relation to women were ever to be assessed, we might well find an organic sickness that has more than contributed to the spiritual death of our times. The face of the whole world has changed since Freud's nativity—and yet women use the same words, go through the same acts, think the same thoughts, dream the same dreams as they did two thousand years ago: only their hemlines have changed. Women can thank Freud for the premature death of their possible new dimensions.

Was Freud a latent homosexual? He was certainly obsessed by the two sides of one idea—obsessed both by the penis and the fact that women did not have one. Either way, his misogyny was rampant. While the Greeks depicted woman as "deficient" Freud made this "deficiency" the nodal point of her existence.

One cannot very well doubt the importance of penis envy [he wrote, without explaining why one could not] doubt it.] Perhaps you will regard the hypothesis that envy and jealousy play a greater part in the mental life of women than they do in that of men as an example of male unfairness. Not that I think their characteristics are absent in man, or that they have no other origin in women except envy of the penis, but I am inclined to ascribe the greater amount of them in women due to the latter influence. (*New Introductory Lectures on Psycho-Analysis*)

Later he was off again:

Their vanity is partly a further effect of penis envy for they are driven to rate their physical charms more highly as a belated compensation for their original sexual inferiority. Modesty . . . was . . . in our opinion, originally designed to hide the deficiency in her genitals. (*New Introductory Lectures on Psycho-Analysis*)

And again in the same lecture series:

The castration complex of the girl is started by the sight of genital organs of the other sex. She immediately notices the difference and—it must be admitted—its significance. She feels herself at a great disadvantage and often declares that she "would like to have something like that," and falls a victim of penis envy which leaves uneradicable traces on her development and character formation.

(Here are two fine examples of Freud defining his own terms to preclude any possible opposition: "Perhaps you will regard the hypothesis . . . as an example of male unfairness," and "Modesty was designed . . ." etc. Freud uses an old ploy: those who question the answer fall instantly into the category of being one of the types under discussion.)

I do not have, never have had, and never will have a penis. But then neither did Freud have a vagina. Today, there is a growing amount of evidence that men envy and stand in awe of the female reproductive powers. Comparatively recent anthropological studies show that primitive societies developed elaborate rites and ceremonies in which to express vagina and breast envy. *All that Freud wrote was in ignorance of this fact.*

Male envy of the female sex organs is the theme of psychologist Bruno Bettelheim's book *Symbolic Wounds: Puberty Rites and the Envious Male.* For this study, Dr. Bettelheim drew from his own observations of a group of schizophrenic adolescents (all about twelve, I.Q.s 115–140, white, and of middle-class origin) and from the firsthand observations of those who had studied primitive societies. It was not his wish to equate the psychotic child and primitive man but merely to express his belief that "all men share certain feelings, desires and anxieties, that these are common not only to various preliterate tribes—as well as to children, psychotic adults and primitive man—but to all of us."

Among the boys, Bettelheim found an intense desire to be able to bear children and the feeling of being cheated because they could not.

> Such intense envy of female sexuality is by no means restricted to women's primary sex apparatus and functions. We have observed several boys tormented by the desire to possess female breasts. The wish to be able to nurse themselves (which they are convinced women can do) was only part of the motive. They were envious of breasts independently of lactation—that is, as sources of power and strength in themselves.

A riddle they repeatedly asked was: "What is the
strongest thing in the world?" And they never failed to
supply the answer: "A brassiere, because it holds two huge
mountains and a milk factory." Girls never seemed interested in the riddle, but the preadolescent emotionally dis-
turbed boys were nearly always fascinated. (*Symbolic
Wounds: Puberty Rites and the Envious Male*)

In an earlier study of younger boys, Bettelheim notes
that:

Each of these boys stated repeatedly, independently of the
other and to different persons, that it felt it was "a cheat"
and "a gyp" that he did not have a vagina. They made remarks such as: "She thinks she's something special because she has a vagina," or "Why can't I have a vagina?"
(*Symbolic Wounds: Puberty Rites and the Envious Male*)

Further data in support of Bettelheim's thesis is supplied
by other psychologists and psychiatrists. M. Chadwick
theorizes that it was man's disappointment with his inability
to create human beings that led him to intellectual creation.
Melanie Klein comments in *Early Stages of the Oedipus
Conflict: Contributions to Psycho-Analysis* that "the femininity complex of men seems so much more obscure than the
castration complex in women, with which it is equally important," and that the boy's identification with the mother
often results in feelings of envy and hatred towards the
woman "for, on account of his wish for a child, he feels
himself at a disadvantage and inferior to the mother." Bettelheim also quotes Gregory Zilboorg's essay on "Masculine
and Feminine" in *Psychiatry VII* (1944). Zilboorg speaks
of the " 'woman envy on the part of man, that is psychoge-

netically older and therefore more fundamental' than penis envy."

In primitive societies breast and vagina envy and the ceremonies that express this envy are seen as an attempt to "share in women's great and secret power of procreation, a gift that only women can bestow because only women possess it." In such societies woman's ability to reproduce relates directly to the overriding concern with fertility, an inevitable concern in terms of these people's utter dependence on multiplication of crops and animals for survival.

Bettelheim notes that:

> During the ceremonies of the Uli cult of New Ireland . . . elaborate male figures called Ulis are carved. They are powerfully proportioned, bearded figures, whose oversized breasts and phalli express the power of fertility, the cult which they serve. They are not viewed as hermaphroditic; on the contrary, they are considered the more male because they also possess female sex powers and characteristics. The ceremonies in which these figures were used sometimes lasted a year, and included dances in which the men tied carved female breasts around their chests. (*Symbolic Wounds: Puberty Rites and the Envious Male*)

It is the practice of subincision that is the most radical attempt to make men physically like women. Ashley Montagu in *Coming into Being* describes the process:

> The operation consists essentially in slitting open the whole or part of the penile urethra along the ventral or under surface of the penis. The initial cut is generally about an inch long, but this may subsequently be enlarged so that the incision extends from the glands to the root of

the scrotum; in this way the whole of the under part of the penile urethra is laid open. The latter form of the operation is universal among the Central tribes (of Australia).

Bettelheim notes that this affects the male's ability to direct his flow of urine; after the operation, the male urinates in a squatting position. What is the deeper meaning of subincision, a voluntary mutilation that is sometimes undergone several times?

Bettelheim suggests:

> If . . . one begins with the fact that the subincision wound is called "vulva," then the operation itself and the repeated opening of and bleeding from the wound become understandable. Then it appears that the purpose of the ritual may be to reproduce symbolically the female sex organ, while the reopening of the wound may symbolize the periodic phenomena of menstruation. Statements made by the people themselves confirm such an interpretation. The Murngin say: "The blood that runs from an incision and with which the dancers paint themselves and their emblems is something more than a man's blood—it is the menses of the old Wawilak women."

From this and other evidence provided by studies of primitive societies, Bettelheim concludes that it is probable that circumcision may have been a male substitute for the first menstruation of girls, and that "subincision was a second attempt to procreate when the first attempt failed."

Imitation of the female extends in some tribes to the male symbolically giving birth. Among those quoted by Bettelheim is Sir E. F. Im Thurn's *Among the Indians of Guiana:*

The woman works as usual up until a few hours before birth; she goes to the forest with some women, and there the birth takes place. In a few hours she is up and at work ... As soon as the child is born, the father takes to his hammock, and abstains from work, from meat and all food but weak gruel of cassava meal, from smoking, from washing himself, and above all, from touching weapons of any sort, and is nursed and cared for by all the women of the place. . . . This goes on for days, sometimes weeks.

Bettelheim suggests that this symbolic act resembles the act of the child who dresses in his parent's clothes—an act of envy and strong attraction to those "in power."

Women, emotionally satisfied by having given birth, and secure in their ability to produce life, can agree to the couvade; men need it to fill the emotional vacuum created by their inability to bear children.

It is interesting that none of this detracts from Bettelheim's total acceptance of the theory of penis envy.

Penis envy is so well known and has been so often described that its universality needs little more discussion.

Later in *Symbolic Wounds: Puberty Rites and the Envious Male:*

If in this book I speak mainly about the male envy of female sex functions this is because it is less often discussed and not because "penis envy" is any less common.

If this phenomenon is as widespread among males as Bettelheim suggests, one must question why Freud did not

observe it among his own male patients. Perhaps Freud was
so steeped in the Greek concept of woman as a "deficient
being" and man as a superior being that it would be outside
his ability to perceive any evidence of male desire to be like
woman; if perceived it would be interpreted not as a norm
but as an aberration.

There is a strong possibility, of course, that neither penis
envy nor vagina envy exists. The word "envy" is the key
word. What Freud perceived might more accurately have
been described as "longing" rather than "envy," in the
sense that women longed for the freedom that came with
possession of the penis. *Envy* is a denigrating word: while
it does not accurately describe the female state of mind,
it reveals much of Freud's state of mind. Whenever he lec-
tured, he came equipped with a little repertoire of stories
less designed to enlighten the audience regarding woman
than to stereotype woman and humiliate her. Here are two
illustrations from a series of lectures entitled: *Group Psychology and the Analysis of the Ego.*

> We have only to think of the troop of women and girls, all
> of them in love in an enthusiastically sentimental way,
> who crowd around a singer or pianist after his perfor-
> mance . . . and instead of pulling out one another's hair . . .

> Supposing that one of the girls in a boarding school has
> just had a letter from someone with whom she is secretly
> in love which arouses her jealousy and she reacts to it with
> a fit of hysteria. . . .

Hysteria, envy, jealousy . . . these were the key characteristics when Freud spoke of women. In the same lecture series

he noted that "women have but little sense of justice and this is no doubt connected with the preponderance of envy in their mental life." All this longing and striving to be something else sprang from the one source—lack of a dick.

Obviously, Freud was as incapable of understanding woman as a Florida cracker is incapable of understanding the black man. The harvest of his mentality is in his writings and nowhere is there a true accounting of the female spirit. There is not a whisper of female intellectuality, spirit, courage, insight, strength, unless it travels along the domestic route of Freud's approval. Like a gynecologist, he sat on a stool for fifty years before an imaginary stirruped woman, his eyes and mind fixated on her vagina. When he got up after fifty years he knew as much about real woman as the day he sat down. One wonders about his female patients whose cases he so meticulously recorded, those poor, wealthy, neurotic middle-class women suffocated by the domesticated roles that were strangling their psychic lives. One wonders why so many of them showed signs of hysteria. Could it not have been more the result of the treatment than the disease? (One recalls a more recent case of female "hysteria" in New York City when a Spanish woman entered a bar to get telephone change. Nobody understood her, she became excited, somebody called the police, she became terrified, the police took her to a hospital, nobody understanding a word, and there she was forcibly held for five days, now in a state of total madness. Only on the fifth day did a social worker visit her tenement home and find two babies dead from thirst in their cots. That was what she had been trying to say. She was listed on the hospital records as a female "hysteric.")

It is in his correspondence with fiancée Martha Bernays that Freud most clearly reveals his male ego's hungering for control and authority. For instance, docile Martha asks whether he minds her skating. "First," he replies, "if I will allow you to skate. Definitely not, I am too jealous for that. ... So drop the idea." Later, Martha writes that she has visited a former girlfriend of whom Freud disapproves. After chiding Martha for visiting a girl of "utter weakness and lack of principle," Freud cautions Martha: "Just you wait, when I come you will soon get used to having a master again."

The reality of Freud's existence *as a man* would surely lie in the authenticity of his relationships with women. Yet there is no evidence that he ever experienced this reality or realized its meaning or importance, or even suspected its existence. Not for a moment in the above excerpts does Freud appear to suspect himself or what his image of a desirable male-female relationship reveals about his own relationship with half the world.

What it reveals leaves no doubt in my mind as to the total irrelevancy of Freud's theories regarding women. His theory of "penis envy," springing from a basic faith in the superiority of the male, is basic to the whole psychiatric scheme to this day. The facts appear to me somewhat differently. Both sexes are drawn to possess one another's attributes, she to possess his penis, he to possess her vagina and breasts. This is not an expression of "envy" but rather proof of the basic dynamic of nature—the drawing together of the opposite and complementary sexes.

All the natural sciences, such as the physics of Maxwell who was a contemporary of Freud, have changed entirely since Freud's day. But Freud's theories are perpetuated: they are timeless because they are proofless. One cannot weigh in a test tube or measure in a charge the element of "penis envy." The modern woman knows this and is on the verge of a total rejection of modern psychiatry. The next decade will see more and more women going to liberation meetings for their therapy rather than to a psychiatrist.

# CHAPTER

# V

It seems some things cannot be said too often, particularly when the saying of them has fallen on stone ears. It has been two decades since Simone de Beauvoir's *The Second Sex* or Mirra Komarovsky's *Women in the Modern World* attempted to destroy the system of raising girls. These were brave efforts but ripe before their time, for the conditioning of the female infant to be "feminized" has been exacerbated rather than ameliorated since. (A higher proportion of women received Ph.D.s in 1920 than will receive them in 1970. The number of women earning master's degrees in 1969 was lower than in 1930. Women today hold thirty-eight percent of all technical and professional jobs as compared to forty-five percent in 1940. And men on the average are paid nearly twice as much as women for all jobs in all economic classes.) Marya Mannes has been another fighter for the building of a new female brain and again the system of raising little girls has been a prime target. So

59

far the struggle has been in vain; where the problem is so vast only a massive victory can be counted as gain.

The problem that these writers have described could be summed up like this: Man imagines that his life is richer by keeping woman in a subservient position. To ensure success, man programs the female child into a domestic role by the age of three. Conditioning to domesticity at such an early age guarantees prolific guilt for the girl who might later attempt to reprogram herself.

This conditioning is accomplished primarily through the toys that are given to the girl-child. Unlike the boy, her toys are limited to a certain function. She is given baby dolls, tea sets, pots and pans, midget ovens, cake mix sets, midget washing machines, midget freezers and midget groceries—everything necessary to develop the midget mind.

None of these toys relate to the realities of the world outside the home. Nor do they offer any variety of life experience to the girl-child. The boy-child, however, through his toys, is offered almost unlimited perceptions and goals. The spectrum of life offered the female child starts at the freezer and ends at the stove. For her, the outside world does not exist. A visit to any toy department illustrates this fact.

All the girl's toys are directed towards a totally subjective relationship with other people. Her stove is a tool by which she bakes for others. Her tea set gives her a chance to show off her skills at entertaining. When she dresses and undresses her doll she puts on garments dictated as suitable by male society. She discovers quickly enough that the play which engenders the greatest parental tenderness is her acting out of being "a lady"—her childish imitation of the narrow, selected and often warped behavior patterns of the female adults who surround her.

As she grows, she becomes more and more father's little pet. He calls her "his little lady" and, more pointedly, "the little mother" as she plays with her "babies." He beams with indulgent amusement at her developing coquettishness, an act that she soon finds is most rewarding with males. It becomes obvious that she is being prepared for a future that hinges on her body. This message is transmitted in a million ways—the care with which her hair is shaped, the ribbons placed on it, the gift of panties and slips embossed with lace and pink roses, the attention that zeroes in on the clothes she wears. She perceives that this future will be largely determined by her prettiness, charm, figure, daintiness—in total, her desirability as a sexual object. By five, the girl child finds herself in the center of a subworld that evolves around her sex organs, a world in which her willingness to conform to the image of "lady" determines her acceptance.

The upbringing of the female child has even deeper, more harmful effects than this conditioning to a life limited to housekeeping. I am referring to the destruction of the child's imaginative faculty—the crippling of her capacity for a full and complete experience of life.

Let us look at what is happening to the boy during these childhood years. At the same time that the horizons opened to the girl are being cut down to the size of a washing machine, the boy is being taught "to act like a man." He is given toys that unfold the spectrum of history, such as bows and arrows and sailing ships, toys that give his receptive young mind some notions of his time and place in history. The train sets, the steam engines, the fire engines and police cars, all act as an aid to his forming a sense of who he is. Few of the toys that he is given are finished toys, unlike those given the girl. He is given a hammer and a few nails and told to go make something, or a shovel and a tool and told to take off.

He is encouraged to engage in competitive sports, to run, play ball, climb through windows, fight his rivals, explore, lift weights, flex his muscles and struggle under burdens. As he projects himself into the wide horizons of his coming adulthood, he realizes that if his life is tougher than that of a girl, it is because he is being prepared for a bigger, tougher and more rewarding future, a future in which his value will not lie in the body but in the mind.

Simone de Beauvoir comes closer than any other analyst in approaching my thesis as to why this system of domestication is self-perpetuating and why women, with all the energy and intelligence necessary, find it an all but impossible task to cross from their interiorized world to exterior realities. Miss de Beauvoir comes close but just misses.

"Woman exhausts her courage dissipating mirages and then stops in terror at the threshold of reality," wrote De Beauvoir in *The Second Sex*. This is an accurate observation of a very important phenomenon, one which any woman in the business or career world has observed a hundred times among her colleagues who have not yet reached that heady degree of success or defiance which in itself creates the necessary energy to thrust one out into the world still further. Yet I reject De Beauvoir's contention that woman stops at reality because of weariness. As a

woman earning a competitive living in the man's world—
and for that matter as a wife and mother—the syndrome of
which De Beauvoir speaks—a total physical and psychological and even spiritual fatigue—is a known factor in my
life. Yet I sense, even in my scarred soul, the traces of an
alibi. Fatigue provides no adequate explanation for this
phenomenon.

The explanation lies in the sad fact that woman has no
imagination. Imagination provides the psychological structure through which one passes from an interiorized life into
the outside world, but woman has been systematically deprived as a child of any opportunity to build that structure.
When she reaches the threshold of reality it is not the lack of
energy that holds her back (unless one chooses to look
upon the imagination as a form of energy and I do not believe De Beauvoir meant that); it is a lack of images and
principles that would help her determine her course of action.

Let us look at a girl in her late teens or early twenties
standing on this threshold of the exterior world. All her life
she has conformed to the anonymous authority of the male
construct. She has suppressed her spontaneous feelings and
so relinquished any chance of individuality. Her head is
filled with ready-made thoughts and a fictitious picture of
the world and its relationships. She has been taught systematically to distrust her own intellectual capacities and has
been sealed off from any experiences that might have been
a nutrient for them. The world awaiting her is a world
dominated by the male and male institutions. It is a world
increasingly dependent on technology, a technology which
is as great a mystery to her as to the cave woman.

Legally, sexually, educationally, this young woman is free to act as she wants, as she thinks, as she pleases and as she feels, but she doesn't know what she wants, or what will please her, or how she feels. It is of great importance to understand why this woman approaching adulthood is overwhelmed by a sense of smallness, doubt and fear.

Her childhood has been spent in a world which systematically excluded her from any involvement in sensation. Sensation is critical to the development of the imagination; indeed, it is the imagination's sole nutrient. Without sensation, the imagination has no means of developing or sustaining life. The mind cannot reproduce what it has never known and what it has known is the basis for all projections and imaginary constructs.

Let us compare the part played by sensation in the lives of both boys and girls.

The girl is neither allowed nor encouraged to explore her bodily strengths through contest, to flex her muscles, lift weights, suffer sunburn, feel the cold, fall down, climb trees, throw balls, kick, race or wrestle, and so develop a bank of sensations as well as a feeling for spatial concepts and balance. The body contacts engaged in daily by boys, whether on the sports field or a tenement street, exclude her. This process, by which the imagination develops, is part and parcel of the daily tumble of life even for the child in the ghetto.

There is another element in the play-life of boys that is lacking in the play-life of girls. This is competitive scrutiny by one's own peer group. The games boys play are competitive games such as football and cops and robbers. They demand a degree of reality and other members of the gang continually scrutinize one another to see if the "pretend" is sufficiently and suitably realistic. Every time a boy pretends to be a cop, there are a number of little friends around ready to beat him on the head, if only with verbal scorn, if his "pretend" is not realistic. This competitive scrutiny plays a comparatively very minor role in the "pretends" of girl-children. Her domestic play is no more subject to meeting harsh, exterior standards of the larger world than is her own mother's housekeeping subject to appraisal by the world at large. The behavior of the housewife domestically is an individual matter; the behavior of the football player, the cop or the robber is not.

In learning to pretend realistically, the boy has been forced to develop a capacity for constructing realistic alternatives to problems. The girl has no such practice; within the confines of her domesticated play, she can make up her own rules. As she develops into a woman, she will have only one answer to everything she does. Rare is the woman who can come up with more than one alternative to a problem. And so woman falls back on her intuition for she is incapable of analysis, incapable of constructing a realistic alternative. It is more than likely that this characteristic inability of women to analyze is not an inborn characteristic but rather the direct result of her narrow and overprotected childhood. If a girl's upbringing were equivalent to that of a boy's, it is possible that the cellular difference, the chromosomal difference, might cause her to perceive realistic alternatives that were different in whole or part from those perceived by a man. But certainly she would be capable of constructing these alternatives and to believe otherwise is to maintain that women are less than human.

There is yet another observable result of this domestication of the girl-child. It is perhaps the greatest deprivation of all deprivations imposed upon her by the adult world in the name of kindness. It destroys not only the girl's ability to deal with the world effectively—to enter into a constructive and spontaneous relationship with the outside world—but it destroys any possibility of authentic communication between male and female. By precluding the experience of sensation from her play, and by limiting her imaginative growth with the type of toys played with, the girl-child is set on a path in which she has comparatively little practice in distinguishing external stimuli from fantasy. That is, as the degree of mental or physical stimulation from the external world is reduced, it becomes increasingly difficult for a person to distinguish fantasy from reality because the degree of stimulation is the only method by which the "now" can be separated from the fantasy.

If one spends one's life in the comparatively bland and languid air of the home, where the challenges are petty and the goal is to survive until the evening's television programs, where there is no competitive scrutiny and consequently no standards that must be met, and where, from day to day, sensations are minimal, fantasy and reality are in danger of interlocking. It is a common and correct observation among men that the female's difficulty in distinguishing fantasy from reality is often monumental.

The lack of imagination, the inability to construct realistic alternatives, and the difficulty in separating fantasy from reality blend together to form man's gift to the capitalist system—the exploited and witless consumer. The essence of excitement for most women is spending money. Cast an eye on daily realities. If women are not to be found at the Vietnam peace talks, in Congress or in the Senate, in the diplomatic service or the World Bank, or managing office departments, or analyzing tax budgets, where are women to be found? In and out of department stores spending billions of dollars. Buying beds, sofas, pots and pans, washing machines, dryers, tables, chairs—buying but rarely designing. Buying airplane tickets but never building a plane. Using the telephone but never installing one. Driving a car but never fixing it. There is no limit to woman's dependency on man. She is incapable of making, designing, even fixing any one of the scores of technical products she uses daily. If any should break down, she is totally dependent on the repair *man* to set things straight. Being a woman, I would like to believe that woman is more capable than this. The woman of the future will be. But as of this moment woman must face the fact that if her refrigerator breaks, her swimming pool blocks, her hair dryer blows out, her television breaks down, her car has a flat, she will be reduced instantly to her true status in this society—a chronically dependent and passive being in an unfamiliar world. Can she claim equality with man when her understanding of twentieth-century technology is little better than that of a peasant in the Middle Ages?

It is a kindness that woman's lack of imagination probably saves her at this juncture from the hideous realization of just how viciously she is exploited. She *cannot imagine* that all detergents are basically the same, that there is only one basic formula for floor wax, that window sprays, dishwasher powders, bleaches, germ killers are all the same.

The same manufacturers make them and, as if dealing with children, create new trade names, billion-dollar advertising campaigns, novel shapes, new colors, all to keep the little lady buying and trying in the fantasy world man has created for her for his own increased monetary profit.

Men laugh at woman because she is so easily duped. She is just not a person to be taken seriously. If he allows her into the multibillion-dollar business of selling, it is to *use* her. To use her as a sex symbol. She is the air hostess who helps sell plane tickets by wearing a dress cut to her thighs, the model in the bikini at the boat show, the secretary with the long legs or cute little bottom. Women have long since faced the fact that men, either by their nature or the construct they have imposed upon themselves, look at an employee's bust or bottom long before, if ever, they think of looking at her brains. The bitterness this arouses in the sensitive woman can hardly be measured; in her sense of degradation she wonders how men would like to have the length of their dick appraised every time they walk through a door seeking an honest job. A large measure of this bitterness springs not from personal affront as much as the sense of being trapped in a man-made psychological apparatus which hones down all females and prepares them for a biological destiny within the home.

It is this apparatus that women must reconstruct or destroy if they are ever to be fully identified with the human. It is this apparatus that acts as a force of oppression and deception, for its true purpose is to create a false sexual differentiation, a differentiation that imposes on all activities concepts of male and female that are intellectual constructs often devoid of any reality.

We can see the importance society invests in its rigid concepts of the sex roles by reversing the situation, by saying it is masculine to be passive, intuitive, irrational, timid, modest, pious; to be a homemaker, nurse, secretary, hairdresser, kindergarten teacher, pool typist. And that it is feminine to be ambitious, competitive, rational, active and exploratory; to be bankers, truck drivers, diplomats, construction workers; to drill for oil, fly planes, build automobiles, join the Armed Services, hunt and fish. With such an illustration it is easy to see how rigid our concepts are in the area of what is "masculine" and what is "feminine." The occupations listed could be done equally well by either sex and in other societies often are.

Earlier the question was asked why so much has been said in recent years about the crippling conditioning women undergo as children and so little done to change it. *The ultimate answer is that it is the present form of capitalism as practiced in most Western societies that motivates and supports this nonproductive, subservient, voiceless role for women. Continued increased productivity with continued increased consumption is the underlying philosophy of capitalism.* Woman does not participate in that productivity yet she is the major consumer.

Again, we return to woman's lack of imagination. The economic system universally is the fruit of the male imagination. Woman's failure to participate in the production of the goods she consumes is the fruit of her lack of imagination. Further, it is the imagination of the male within the capitalist system that continually conjures up new products as well as new methods of convincing woman that she needs that product.

Now this convincing takes many forms yet one must insist
it is no accident that the prime tool used by the male commercial world to sell its products is the biological guilt of
the female, that psychic composite that springs from a life
lived in false style.

Consider this advertisement as one example. Under a
hazy picture of a sweet young girl sitting on the compliant
sand dunes (*that* was no accident) with her knees suitably
drawn up, the caption states:

"Unfortunately, the trickiest deodorant problem a girl
has isn't under her pretty little arms. *That* was solved long
ago. The real problem, as you very well know, is how to
keep the most girl part of you—the vaginal area—fresh
and free of any worry-making odors.

"Now, finally, there is a way. It's called _____, a brand-
new vaginal spray deodorant that's been especially developed to cope with the problem. It works externally, because
that's where the trouble starts. Tension and pressure can
cause it. So can getting all hot and perspiry. So can your
own natural body functions. No matter. Whatever starts
these troublesome odors, _____ stops them effectively. And
nicely. And very, very gently . . . it protects you, calmly
and quietly, for hours.

"Why take chances? Make _____ as much a part of your
daily life as your bath or shower. It's just as essential to
your cleanliness. *And to your peace of mind about being a
girl.* An attractive, nice-to-be-with girl."

There is a measure of contempt for the female mind and
body here that is almost limitless. To be a woman is at
once to be smelly—the basic premise of the advertisement.
Further, it is "the most girl part" that is the most reprehen-

sible part. Not the armpits or the small of the back or the legs; men share these physiological attributes. No, it is the "most girl part"; apparently, the reality cannot bear closer description. Impossible to escape the image of something small, black and furry, rather like a housepet that is yet to be broken. There is an aura of affection for this "most girl part" while there is a clear acknowledgment that the same part is at once unreliable, leaky and likely to stink up the room. If it cannot be trained, it can at least be controlled by systematic aerosol attacks. This saturation bombing is essential to "one's peace of mind about being a girl," for by now it should be understood that to be born a girl is to be born with a defect. It is no accident that this defect is an absence—the absence of a penis——and into this vacuum some spray must fall.

To spray one's vagina as if it were harboring fleas is to express in one form an implacable fear of one's own being, an alienation from and distrust of one's most intimate self. A nonacceptance of self, in fact, that verges on loathing. Yet I am certain that across the nation women are now spraying their vaginas with religious regularity; if they all did it together the pressure would likely blow the nation apart. There is no reason to believe otherwise.

Caught within a psychological and commercial structure built by man for reasons that include commercial gain, woman's self-distrust has been honed already to such a point that she covers her hair with one spray, her breath with another, her armpits with another, her body with another. And now her vagina is being dusted; it took the aerosol giants one decade to get there.

This advertisment is a superb fruit of the male imagination. Working within the capitalist system, with the sole aim of increased productivity, he has conjured up not only another new product that is viciously criminal in a world where one-third of the inhabitants are slowly starving. But he has managed to conjure up from an old male rationale —that there is something dirty and unclean about the sexuality of women—some new imagery. He knows from experience that a little scolding on the subject of cleanliness goes a long way with women and that in the flaccid world of the housewife the deepest issue has become the eradication of dirt. The fact that this campaign is costing more female souls than were ever lost in the Black Plague is not of interest to him. All that was of interest was to find a new element in female psychology that could be made vulnerable to guilt. And he found it.

# CHAPTER

# VI

Total fulfillment in a domestic role is not only possible but is a fact of achievement for an unknown number of women. The existence of such women was ignored in Betty Friedan's contribution, *The Feminine Mystique,* which dealt, and properly, with the realities as they are experienced daily by millions of others. But Friedan's conclusion that *all women* would find happiness and fulfillment in work outside the home runs counter to my own observations and is unacceptable. There are many women who under no circumstances would wish to leave their homes to take outside employment no matter how challenging or rewarding that employment might be. Many of these women have good to high I.Q.s and college degrees and are not only fulfilled physically and sexually but blossom psychologically and spiritually over the years as courageous and worthwhile human beings. Domesticity is the humus by which these women grow and the fruit of this growth is often a rare depth and perceptivity. In a love-starved and restless society, these qualities are of enormous value. It is my observation, however, that such women come from homes that appear to be free of gross financial or psychological stress—where there is an assured income, if a modest one, and/or their husbands are basically kind and considerate men. The idea, so beloved in fiction, that woman can blossom spiritually in a home that is stressful—for whatever reason—is romantic rubbish. (I would concede, however, that genuine sublimation would be possible in some rare cases, possibly where the woman is authentically religious.)

*The Feminine Mystique,* nonetheless, went ten miles deeper into reality than Phyllis McGinley's *Sixpence in My Shoe,* a prime example of insensitivity to all reality but the author's own. In describing how making a custard was as challenging as writing a poem, Miss McGinley chose to ignore the fifty other inputs that comprised this sense of satisfaction. For instance, the international recognition bestowed upon her as a Pulitzer Prize winner in poetry, marriage to a successful stockbroker husband, a fine country home, etc., etc. More important than any of these material achievements was a reward towards which she appears totally insensitive—the excitement and satisfaction generated by growth in her craft and the magnificent anticipation of an unknown and exciting future. Many of the pleasures which most women know only through their dreams were already securely hers as she stirred her custard. She failed to see that cooking was a pleasure because it was a hobby, not a tedious and worrisome necessity squeezed out of a pinched budget. Nor was it the high point of the day's existence; if it flopped she could give it to the cat and go out for dinner. Miss McGinley had alternatives to her existence.

In scolding women who were unhappy because they did not have the freedom these alternatives bestowed, she simply betrayed the distance between her life and the lot of most women.

McGinley is an extreme example of the many women and men who, because they themselves do not suffer or are unaware of their suffering, do not seem to recognize the problems endured by others. I do not believe with Friedan that the one answer to this problem of slow death by domestication lies in outside employment. Obviously, it is critical at this point in history that the majority of women enter into a far more realistic and constructive relationship with the outside world but the mode in which this relationship operates is not my prime concern. I do not care whether women work or do not work. What is important is that women be freed from the network of false imagery and hypocrisy that at present destroys so much female creative energy and raises such obstacles to spontaneous and authentic love between male and female and mother and child. I am particularly concerned with those few women who are authentically creative, and with that other large segment of unremarked and unknown women who cannot hope for a life of normal rewards and stability unless they are free to guiltlessly seek and enjoy work outside their homes. I am referring to those many women who are married to cold, unloving brutes; to egotistical maniacs; to alcoholics; to the chronically depressed; the sexually perverted; the total economic failures; the jealous neurotics; the gamblers. Any priest, psychiatrist or social worker would vouch that the world is full of such wrecks and each one of them belongs to a woman. It is all very well to say that no woman should live with such a man but the fact is that women do and often love them. (Note that if a woman stays with such a spouse she is labeled "masochistic": if a man stays with such a spouse he is labeled as "dedicated" or "committed.") For such a woman, work outside the home is essential to her psychological well-being. And if this woman can find employment, or if she is the truly creative woman we spoke of above, or simply if she enjoys work and is a better wife and mother because of outside employment, then she should be totally free to work and should be assisted by society at large to do so. If she wishes to stay at home, she should be just as free to do so without being automatically labeled as a brainwashed victim of domestication.

The fundamental question is not whether women should or should not work; whether women are inferior or superior to men; whether certain industries treat them fairly or unfairly, although such specifics are part of the overall picture. The basic question is how best to remove or restructure those psychological forces which prevent women from acting as a strong and constructive social force. I believe that when these barriers are removed the specific difficulties which women experience in employment and legal and social matters will dissipate. This sequence is the reverse of what many feminists advocate but I believe it is the only workable one.

A case in point. At the time of this writing, I am temporarily living on a university campus in housing for faculty and postgraduate students. The total facilities of the university are no more than half a mile away—yet out of 100 wives in this block only one of them is taking an academic course. All are young, all have their lives before them; most have two or three children but free babysitting facilities are readily available. It is a frequent cry that education is the route to the outer world for women, that there should be a variety of programs offered at suitable times and places to the wife and mother. Specific job training at university level does present a real difficulty for married women but that is not our concern here. Rather, it is the question of a lively and continuing intellectual curiosity, a desire for growth. But the evidence all around me indicates there is none. One can only ask, looking at the women who now surround me, how accessible does college have to be before women will participate? Even a sympathetic woman cannot deny that, granted higher education, women have refused to take advantage of it. There is nothing unique in the situation that now surrounds me; if young married women have no interest in learning now it is merely because they had no interest before marriage. So it is with the vote: woman has knocked over many a would-be rescuer in her attempt to get back to the playpen.

The question of the "woman problem" is not a question of an increase of employment opportunities and legal rights as much as a question of removing psychological blocks. Domestication in the critically formative years is the biggest block of all. In this process of domestication is included all the imagery and expectations which the outside world imposes upon the woman. Returning after a lengthy digression to our initial theme, I am going to give two reasons why woman should destroy this last remnant of the concubinage system. We will first discuss the psychological effects on the female, then on her society—two horns on the same cow, as it were.

When a woman is born the stage is set for her just as it is

for man. To survive, she must comply with certain conditions. Man goes into a world where all the rules have been set out by male institutions; the woman must accept these institutions although every cell in her body—and perhaps as a result her concepts and perceptions—is somewhat different from the male. In addition to her acceptance and adherence to the authority of the male institutions, she must also conform to the male construct of what is "feminine" and what is "unfeminine." In other words, she is taught how to be a woman by man.

The expression of spontaneous thought and of individual likes and dislikes is an essential ingredient of the human growth process. But while the young man is taught to engage and struggle with the outside world, it is impressed upon young women that they are most feminine if they are spectators, rather than participants. Or at best, pseudo-participants until one of the young and aggressive bulls (or better yet, a rich old bull) carries her back to the safety and security of the home.

Among these female children programmed into domesticity as infants there will be some who will arrive at a total integration of themselves in the role of wife and mother. But what of the other young girl whose drives for self-growth, individuation and self-realization travel in the antithetical direction—the girl who does not like dolls, is competitive, active, ambitious, who is bored by babies and mad for travel? What happens to her at that point in womanhood when she is ready to leave home and go into the outside world? She is certainly not adequately prepared, since all her life she has been trained to be somebody other than herself, to curb her own expression and act out the

male construct of woman. Two alternatives present themselves to her. She can at this point start on the grueling task
of breaking with her past; her goal will be to affirm her
own value, create her own true identity and bring from the
depths of her unique self the gift of her contribution, whatever that might be. Or she can accept defeat. If the world
which now stands before her is too threatening, the cost of
growth too painful, she can return to the primary ties which
she so recently left. She can find a man to replace the pater-
nal authority and, through marriage and her new keeper,
recapture the security and warmth she knew as a child.
This will involve the denial of certain inborn impulses and
the acceptance of the image of motherhood others shaped
for her. In the first flush of new wifehood and motherhood,
this will seem a cheap price to pay for the flight from self
and the amelioration of loneliness. But the hidden cost sits
awaiting the passage of time and the ripe moment to demand payment. Erich Fromm deals with this mechanism in
*Escape from Freedom:*

> The amount of destructiveness in individuals is proportion-
> ate to the amount to which expansiveness of life has been
> curtailed. By this we do not mean individual thwartings
> or frustrations but the thwarting of the whole of life, the
> blockage of spontaneity of the growth and expression of
> man's sensuous, emotional and intellectual capacities . . .
> Destructiveness is the outcome of unlived life.

Fromm is speaking here of a life-long process of daily
frustration, of forces that pound to be let out for twenty,
thirty or forty years, of creative impulses that fall into stale
and atrophying air, of ambition that is derided and hope

that is never fulfilled. He is speaking of forces that have been buried alive within the body: they cannot be defeated for they are an integral part of the person's being; they die only at the final bodily death.

Betty Friedan writes of the woman whose frustrated drives for growth and self-realization are channeled into hostility towards all those surrounding her, particularly the husband and children. The wife and mother sees these as the objects responsible for her death-in-life and it is at them she strikes. For outsiders she may keep up her image of happiness and success; from those most close she extracts the price. It is a common phenomenon. Observe the women around you. As teenagers they were bright, capable, laughed as readily as they spoke, seemed to be filled with potential, were avid for new adventures. What happened to these girls in the twenty years that followed? Where is the bright, laughing teenager in the glowering wife screaming at her three-year-old or in the matron waiting sullenly for her husband to come home, her heart a bag of grievances? Where is her capability, her brightness, her laughter, her warmth? No matter what the individual aspects of their lives, the one common characteristic of so many married women is simply a lack of joy. Their joy has been destroyed as they realized slowly that this was it, this was to be their life and they hated it.

The enormous value of Friedan's work was that it brought this despair to the surface. That this hidden despair has long existed I have no doubt; even Charles Darwin obliquely refers to it. Darwin's grandfather, a Harley Street surgeon, had expressed astonishment at the number of "suitably married" matrons who crowded his surgery with nonexistent physical complaints; their real complaints were hearts that were breaking with a deep unhappiness and sense of worthlessness. Undoubtedly, there have always been women who have had to confront the terrible realization that their lives have been wasted. But never has the problem been so widespread and so conscious. And this is a reflection not so much of a mere increase in numbers or of our continuing exposure to mass-media feedback, but rather of the fact that women now have a variety of alternatives to happily fill the days of their lives. It is this realization that corrodes the lives of so many older women: they married and bore children unaware of alternatives. They go back and search through their college grades with a sense of astonishment as if looking into the diary of a stranger; they look at their bodies and feel their strength; they look at their career-oriented contemporaries and suspect their inborn talents to be no greater than their own. But they have aborted their own talent whereas their contemporaries have brought theirs to full term and this afflicts them with a sick and jealous grief.

And so these women have no chance to grow although the physical opportunities exist (as I observed in the case of the faculty and postgraduate wives who now surround me). Their chance to grow is destroyed by a psychological barrier—the denial of themselves through youthful marriage that was primarily a means of escape has made it imperative for them to conform to the most rigid images of "femininity." Such women can be sure of themselves only if they live up to the expectations of others. How many readers had mothers or aunts who lived in terror "of what the neighbors might think"? Only by a scrupulous fulfillment of this "feminine" image can a feeling of security be built and inner doubts silenced. The more women conform to these outside authorities and the less they believe in them, the more powerless they feel and the more forced to conform.

Erich Fromm, again in *Escape from Freedom,* says that the self is strong only as it is active and that spontaneous activity is the only way in which a human being can overcome the terror of aloneness without sacrificing the integrity of self.

*The inability to act spontaneously, to express what one feels and thinks, and the necessity to present a pseudo-self to others, are the roots of inferiority and weakness.*

There could be no more accurate description of the genesis of the "woman problem." It follows that spontaneous activity is the answer to woman's search for true freedom. This activity can be expressed either in love or work. In either case the foremost component of this spontaneity is love, but not "love as the dissolution of the self in another person, not love as the possession of another person, but love as spontaneous affirmation of others, as the union of the individual with others on the basis of the preservation of the individual self," as Fromm defines it. But how can women achieve this spontaneous activity when they have been drilled from infancy in the concept that the acid test of true femininity is not individuation but conformity, and that the true wife and the best mother is she who dissolves her personal being for the good of husband and children?

This concept of spontaneous activity as a means of unit-

ing oneself with the outer world brings us to my second reason for advocating the immediate destruction of the system
of domesticating girls.

Three decades from now the world population will have
doubled. From three and a half billion people today—one-
third of whom are already hungry and malnourished—the
population will rise to six and a half to seven billion. The
population of the United States will go from 200 million to
nearly 300 million. California, as an example of one specific area, will double its present seventeen million population within the next ten years. Every year Los Angeles
spreads out into another seventy square miles. At the end of
this century, a type of Los Angeles will spread from Mexico to the Oregon border. On the East Coast, out of Boston
and down through New York to Washington, then thrusting
out in a thinning triangle to Chicago, 200 million Americans will live in a megalopolis of concrete.

The whole world will be a network of slums, according
to the Thirty-fourth American Assembly, Columbia University, which met in New York in late 1968 to discuss
means of "Overcoming World Hunger." Not only will twice
as much food be needed—and this estimate is based on the
assumption that millions will be allowed to starve slowly as
is being done today—but the quality of food produced will
have to be upgraded. An unknown number of millions
today are receiving inadequate protein in their diet and this
retards full brain development. *While the quantity of mankind explodes in its growth, the quality of mankind is skid-
ding backwards.* Millions of nonfunctioning human beings
are being produced today throughout the world and no

matter what protein resources are tapped in the future, it will be too late for these unknown millions because this retardation can never be reversed.

This acceleration in the rate of population growth "is the most ominous feature of our day." I quote a speaker at that Assembly, Professor Frank W. Notestein, former professor of demography at Princeton University. Even if efficient birth-control systems were implemented immediately, some of the consequences of this explosion are inevitable. Dr. Notestein noted that in underdeveloped countries it takes twenty-seven years to double the per capita income while only twenty-nine years to double the population.

A more typical situation is that in which the total income is rising by 4 percent which, with 2.4 percent population growth, lifts per capita income by only 1.6 percent. In the time it takes per capita income to rise from $200 to $400 the population has increased threefold.

The search for food will be but one imperative in these coming decades. Almost as desperate will be the search for water, clean air, housing, sewage disposal, employment, police protection and medical facilities. It is hard to open the mind to the possibility that such conditions could dominate the life-style of the star-spangled United States. We tend to take it for granted that when such doom is propagated it will be limited to India and China.

It is possible that the United States, Canda, Australia and a handful of other fortunate countries will escape the dead-eye of the Apocalypse with a sufficiency of grain, but grain, as we have stated, is but one aspect of the coming crisis. This can best be illustrated by remarking on one fact. The United States in 1970 has a population of 200 million in a world of three and a half billion. Yet she consumes from thirty-five percent to fifty percent of the world's total resources. When the world's population has doubled, what percentage of the world's resources will the United States be able to garner for herself? With a doubled population she will need 100 percent of all the world's resources just to maintain her present standard of living. Realistically, the most the United States can hope for is to hold onto her present thirty-five to fifty percent share of the world's resources and spread it thinly throughout her doubled population. Perhaps the authorities will set aside small plots in each city and town where the masses can visit and gape and wonder if it were true that once Americans lived like this —in the luxury of a split-level suburban home, where a car was permitted, food was not rationed, water flowed from the tap and was not distributed daily, where flowers actually grew and there was a patch of green lawn, and one could have a baby without a state license.

If we choose to ignore the present realities of population growth and so close our eyes to the possibilities of the future, we will go on programming little girls into the belief that only by running a house and bearing babies can they vindicate their existence and find fulfillment. To do so, we will have to close our eyes to the despair these children will realize in their womanhood when their homes will be limited to two rooms and bearing a child will be openly acknowledged as a socially destructive act. They will have been programmed into a myth. If forgiveness is important, it is likely they will never forgive us.

It is a fact that the future is unknowable, that, in the words of Professor Notestein, "it is all too probable that between now and the end of the century there will be a full-scale war between major powers in which modern engines of destruction will kill a substantial portion of the human race." But who can raise her child on this theme of insanity, a theme that with time might assume an aspect of hope; for only if it eventuates is one vindicated in teaching one's sons and daughters to increase and multiply.

At this point in this complex matter all our previous thoughts begin to coalesce. We have freely admitted that there are some women who are completely fulfilled at home and who give effortlessly to their men and children a quality of serenity and love that is an invaluable contribution to wider society. We have seen—and the evidence presented in *The Feminine Mystique* assuredly supports these observances—that there are millions of other women who are basically as loving and basically as constructive but their inborn characteristics are such that life within the four walls of a home metamorphoses them into hostile and destructive beings.

Both these types of women were raised to find fulfillment within the home. The domestic forces have brought fulfillment to one and psychic havoc to the other. At the same moment that society needs to cut a swathe through the population growth merely to survive, the female sex is being offered any number of alternative life-styles. The time has not only come, it is past due when marriage and motherhood as a life's goal should be cut out of the training of the female child. The concept that woman as mother is closer to the "divine" than woman as scientist should be ruthlessly destroyed. The giving of dolls should be abandoned just as many women have refused to give their young sons guns, for one is proving just as destructive as the other. Mother's Day should be abandoned for what it is—a commercial enterprise—and in its place we should substitute a day of mourning for the one-third of the world's people who go to bed in the pain of hunger every night of their lives. When those around us produce three, four and five children, all the while declaiming their love of children, we must, no matter what the pain caused, refuse to accept such thoughtlessness in silence. It has become imperative that we speak before woman, kept in ignorance by man for so long, destroys the world. The day has come when motherhood should be the lot and privilege of a select minority.

Margaret Sanger, that extraordinary warrior, beautiful woman and mother of two beloved sons, said it all fifty years ago. In *Woman and the New Race* she wrote:

War, famine, poverty, and oppression of the workers will continue while woman makes life cheap. They will cease only when she limits her reproductivity and human life is no longer a thing to be wasted.

And with an insight that was prophetic—for these were times when nobody had heard of smog, pollution or ecology, and atomic power was merely an unharnessed spark in Einstein's brain—Sanger wrote:

Diplomats may formulate leagues of nations and nations may pledge their utmost strength to maintain them, statesmen may dream of reconstructing the world out of alliances, hegemonies and spheres of influence, but woman, continuing to produce explosive populations, will convert these pledges into the proverbial scraps of paper.

My readers might be interested to know that after reading the above, I went to my copy of the *Encyclopaedia Britannica* to find out just when and how often Sanger was arrested by New York police for spreading birth-control information. My copy is the 1911 edition with additions added to the Index in 1922. But the only Sanger mentioned is a John Sanger. Owner of an English circus, he was given seventeen lines.

Sometimes nothing stands for everything.

# VII

There are no bystanders in any revolution and the coming revolution in the world of women will be no exception. Men and women are already lining up in a way which indicates that the instinctive dialectic might well prove to be more concerned with love and hate, you-me, I-Thou relationships than with immediate exterior concerns such as job discrimination.

The truth is simply that a deep antagonism exists between the sexes and before there can be even a beginning of a new psychology of the male-female nexus, this antagonism must be brought up to the surface and all its dimensions examined.

A fruitful area to examine is that of male and female images as projected by television and magazine advertising simply because the male possesses an almost total control of the mass media, hence of the images that are projected. Immediately, one is struck by the fact that the woman over thirty has been annihilated. The only evidence of her existence in the mass media is an occasional freak taking an orgiastic pleasure in the whiteness of her wash or the sticking power of her dentures. If the tapes of television commercials were to be the sole prime source material for future anthropologists they would be excused for believing that the brains of the American woman over thirty were so addled by the strain of washing as to be just a niche above plant life. There is scarcely an advertisement that is not dedicated to proving female bankruptcy. Whether on television or magazines the image of the over-thirty woman is interchangeable and vegetative. If she is sold a car, it is so she can fill it with a maximum of children with a minimum of screaming. Almost all advertisements relating to the house would do credit to Sigmund Freud, so fixated are they on the alleged characteristic of female jealousy. One woman is sick with rage at the whiteness of her neighbor's wash; another's Neanderthal jaw drops to her knees at the sight of her neighbor's floor; another brays like an ass at the sight of her neighbor's baking.

If there is a single factor that has exacerbated the modern woman's confusion as to who she is and what value she has it is her image as projected by the advertising industry. This image has nothing to do with her reality. Instead, one gets either "The Anxious Housewife" image or the ad man's other invention (and his ideal), "The Beautiful People," all those long-legged, sexy, sun-tanned, sullen-lipped rich heterosexuals and homosexuals who sell automobiles, cigarettes and clothing on the power of illusion. The middle-aged and older woman has been wiped out as effectively as if she were gassed. Underlying the cult of Youth and Beauty there is an obsessive fear of all reality and so any

face or body that is more real than unreal is consigned to
the ash heap.

But the images projected by advertising create no hurtful
identification problem for the male. He has seized all the
best ones for himself. There are some advertisements where
he is made to look retarded, but the greater emphasis by far
is on the male as a tough-fibered adventurer, independent,
sardonic, entertaining. At the same age *she* is an old bag fit
only for washing his dirty linen and dishes. When *he*
consumes—and he is being quickly reduced to the same
consumer status as woman—it is at least with a modicum
of dignity. He is the fifty-year-old on horseback with a lined
and leathery face and set jaw, riding the tamed mare and
enjoying a smoke at the same time. He is the gray-haired
middle-aged adventurer in the shining fastback sweeping
across the desert spaces, bright-eyed and expectant with the
promise of now being a better hunter assured of better sex.

If he is sold shaving soap, hair oil, clothes, the image
projected is of sports, vitality, charm.

"Duncan Andrews is doing everything for his hair. Everything wrong," says the Pantene ad. And here comes
Duncan Andrews, booted in leather like a veritable aristo-
crat, the lord and master, and naturally astride a mare. He
is grim-faced, aging, bearded and balding. But he is a male
and all the signs of aging and decay matter not a whit. On
the contrary, they are evidence of wealth, power, sexuality.

If a male uses Pub cologne, it will "uncork a lusty life."
Smirnoff vodka promises to "put a swash in your buckle,"
while Burley cologne starts "the kind of fire a woman can't
put out." Arden's after-shave puts a man on a surfboard in
a roaring, tropical sea whereas Pinaud merely puts a nubile

Oriental girl, attired in an unbuttoned shirt and nothing else, on the nearest chaise longue.

What does our society promise woman through advertising once *her* muscles begin to sag? Is there anywhere any inference that she can back up and become the 100-pound beach girl in a bikini, that she can go roaring over the surf at fifty, that she can go where the action is, that she can seek peace in Marlboro country? Obviously, she can go to hell. She is now the motherly, passive, deadly dependent creature that man intended her to be. That's why he buys the fastback in the first place—to get away from her.

My point is that this society makes no attempt to give women over thirty the illusion that they are either worthy intellectually or worthy being hunted sexually. Woman faces the fact that she reaches her peak at twenty, but that once her hymen has been punctured, her sexual capacities established, and her skin begins to wrinkle, in the public image she has no place to go but down and fast. As a person, she no longer exists. She is a consumer and, like the old plantation hand, destined merely to fade away. Yet man, through his advertising, has prolonged indefinitely that period of life when he is of value, importance and beauty, when he can hunt and all will understand his need for love and recognition.

There is nothing new in this imbalance, which in its essence springs from the importance that man invests in female, but not male, virginity. For instance, there has never been a great male lover in Hollywood films under the age of forty; most reached their peak as screen lovers well after their fifties. Every time Clark Gable took a girl she was twenty-five at the most; by forty she had disappeared. One of the most successful novels in recent years was *Lolita*, the story of an aging man's attraction for a popsicle-licking teenager. Humbert Humbert might have ended up in San Quentin doing twenty years in real life but the combination in fiction of the young virgin and the old bull made for an assured success.

The same dichotomy between the male and female image exists in every aspect of the glossy magazines. While the women's magazines come on like a monthly examination of conscience, to be read preferably in a kneeling position, the boys' magazines (gray-haired, balding and paunchy, they are still boys at heart) are lined up in a clear-cut, unproblematic show of roaring confidence. Their pages thrust out an image of the male as predatory, aggressive, commanding and successful and the fact that most men are none of these things is quite irrelevant. Not for the American male are the aimless pages of innocuous preoccupation with self that splatter the women's magazines. There is no questioning man as he plays out his traditional role of master and conqueror on the glossy pages. There is nary a hint of an article dedicated to working over *his* body and *his* mind for the benefit of the female in particular and the world in general. Despite his equal responsibility in the reproductive act and its consequences, there is no flagellation of self over whether he is a good father, spends enough time with the kids, whether he communicates adequately with his teenagers, whether he is an attractive husband, whether he contributes things other than money in making his house a true home. Nor is there any question as to what percentage of his life should be devoted to his career and what to his family, or when it is desirable or undesirable for his family's sake to get out of the rat race and become a human being. The fact that he is a male eliminates all such ambiguities. As a man he is entitled to give his talents and ambitions free reign and whether or not he enriches or destroys his family in the process is strictly his affair. It is not a subject for public debate.

Another dichotomy between the male and female image exists in the employment market, where the man's maturity and experience are considered assets. When a woman seeks employment, her employability is often closely related to her sexual attractiveness.

Unless a woman's talents are rare she is over the hill at thirty. The Help Wanted column of any newspaper makes this clear. It is true that men, too, are phased out of the labor market long before their natural time but this phasing out does not relate to his body so much as the realities of the labor market. The process of employment selection imposed upon women is far more personal, relating far more to the signs of youth and beauty, or lack of it, than to her proven ability. At that age when sagging muscles and graying hair denote experience in the male, it is the death knell to the woman who has not yet attained the position to which she aspired, or to which her qualifications entitled her. So it is that the older employed woman loses the courage to fight for her rights, while her job-seeking contemporary will seek employment with a knot in the pit of her stomach, fearful that one glance will dismiss her and burning with the fore-knowledge that among the bulk of the staff all her application will generate is uninterest.

As for the younger woman, she goes to her job interview with the same sense of excitement, the same care in doing her hair, make-up and self-examination as if she were going on a date. She knows, and the employment agencies hammer it in, that the real points to be earned in her interview will not come from her typing speed or ability to take shorthand. Should her skills be sufficient, it is the shape of her legs or the curve of her bosom that will settle the issue.

Both younger and older women will be subjected to a type of questioning that nobody would dream of asking the male. The young woman will be asked whether she has a boyfriend; whether she is planning on getting married; how many children does she want. If she is in her mid-twenties or older she will be asked why she has not married. The widow or divorcée will be asked why she has not remarried. And the married woman will be told that, being married, she could not have the dedication required by the position.

The discrimination practiced against the intellectual woman, the academic or highly trained technician, is as vicious if usually more subtle. She will be told: "We had a woman once and she just didn't work out." Or: "The reason we won't give this position to a woman is that we feel women should not be going home so late at night." Or: "We have a woman already." Or: "One of the nice things about you is that you don't look intellectual." Or, following employment: "You don't need a raise as a married woman; some of the men here have a family to support."

More discriminatory than the questioning is the process of job classification. Throughout the United States and Canada, job classification provides the means by which federal, state, municipal and private employers evade adherence to the Civil Rights Act (1964) of the United States and the Human Rights Bill (1969) of Canada. There is nothing to stop an employer from keeping his expenses to the minimum by reducing the classification into which new female employees are placed. There is wage equality only at the office-girl/office-boy base. As the salaries slowly rise the classifications diverge. In hospital employment, women are aides, men are orderlies; women are ward-maids, men are cleaners. In offices, women are payroll clerks, men are bookkeepers; women are acting bookkeepers, men are department heads. In newspaper offices, women are reporters, men are editors; women are woman's page editors, men are political columnists and news analysts. At university level, women are lecturers, research assistants, associate or assistant professors; men are full professors, department heads, chairmen of policy committees and members of boards of trustees.

The truth is that men feel the presence of women in "their" world can be justified only if that presence acts as a satisfying stimulant to the male ego. That the male is rigidly prejudiced against woman entering a field where she would not play an ego-supportive role is illustrated by the attitude towards women as commercial pilots. There are all-woman airline crews in Russia; Swedish airlines employ women either as pilots or copilots; and a recent picture of mainland Chinese fighter pilots shows a scattering of women graduates. But there are no women employed as commercial pilots in the United States despite the number who are qualified. We have been so brainwashed about the "inborn" inability of all women to make calculated, analytic decisions that both male and female passengers would be susceptible to the same panic should a gray-haired woman, wearing the four gold stripes of captain, walk down the aisle of an American airliner to take over the controls.

What a spiritual crisis would ensue! The supremacy of the male is not merely a social attitude; it is a matter of faith and dogma. And the real guardians of this faith are the major industries. The more technically advanced, the greater the need to cling to the faith of their fathers. In fact, it has been the major airlines that have made the most distinctive contribution to maintaining a double standard, in this case a moral double standard. Until late 1968 no stewardess could marry. She could live with a man and could become pregnant, in which case she would be given full leave and maternity benefits. But she could not marry and give her child the father's name should she wish. For that would jeopardize the billion-dollar image of the un-touched, decorous but more-than-ready virgin hostess.

This is the ambiance in which most women work and if the sincere male wishes to know one reason why so many women hate men, I would suggest that he investigate the employment situation a little further.

In attempting to pinpoint specific areas which give rise to hate and tensions between male and female, the comparison is often made between the position of the woman and that of the black. This mode of thinking has historical roots.

Back in 1848 when feminist leaders met in Seneca Falls to formulate their program they stated that "the whole theory of the Common Law in relation to woman is unjust and degrading, tending to reduce her to a level with the slave. . . . She can do nothing, having nothing which is not regarded by the law as belonging to her husband. Slaves are we, politically and legally. The first women's group in the United States in fact was formed to fight slavery. The sense of identification with the black man under the auctioneer's gavel was so deep that the historic 1848 meeting came five years after an abortive attempt by the same nucleus of women to start a nationwide antislavery movement.

The comparison of the black with the white woman is not a valid comparison—at least neither more nor less than a comparison of the white woman with the Jews or any other minority group. To be black is not to be female and to be female is not to be black. Blackness and femaleness are different existential realities. Yet, the comparison is of more than passing interest in these times because the essence of its expression is an exposure of the white male viewpoint and an exposure of the techniques used to keep the black and the female subservient.

The most potent technique of the white male is the formation of a schema of stereotypes. (The most effective medium for this is the advertising industry.) In her brilliant book, *Thinking about Women,* Mary Ellman lists the characteristics of these stereotypes as formlessness, passivity, insatiability, confinement, piety, materiality, spirituality, irrationality, compliancy, plus the two incorrigible figures of The Shrew and the Witch. I couldn't do better than that. If we line this female stereotyping against that of the black, we find a curious similarity.

Even positive stereotypes are designed to indicate a negative aspect. If we say that woman is spiritual, we find that the black has soul. Both spirituality and soul become substitutes for brains. It's a foolproof method of attack. Incapable of analytic thought, both woman and black drift along receiving all the intellectual nutrient they need from Mother Earth and Jungle Heat. Devoid of intelligence, they lack goals or true stability. God bless them though, black and bitch; they are pious creatures, easily made happy with a pat on the butt or a bottle of booze at Christmas. Both are passive and confined, within the plantation as it were. And both fitfully struggle against a natural indolence and aimlessness.

Only by reinforcing this concept of aimlessness is it possible to maintain another old saw—that ambition is most reprehensible in both black and woman. Today the heat is off the black who is ambitious, but this is not so with women.

No matter how passionate and giving in her private life, the woman who reveals ambition will not only run up against harsh intra-office sanctions denying this ambition but will be struck with the searing label of "frigid." (Note that women are "frigid," which has a moral connotation of reprehensible coldness of soul while men are "impotent," which has a physical connotation of a human in distress.) All the exteriorities of the ambitious woman will be judged in a sexual context. At no time will her ambition be perceived for what it is—the natural thrust of a passionate and creative soul. If she wears her hair short and her clothing tailored, she is "masculine." If she wears her hair long and her clothes frilly, she is using sex to get ahead. If she puts in long hours at the office, it is because she hasn't a boyfriend and is probably a lesbian. If she doesn't stay at the office, it is because she is sleeping with the boss.

By attacking the ambitious woman in this or a similar manner, the supremacist male takes a further revenge: he degrades the man in this woman's life, and this is a tactic against which no woman has any effective redress. As the supremacist really believes that the male owns the female, body and soul, he views the time and the energy which the ambitious woman puts into her job as stolen from the poor sap who got himself tangled up with her. The supremacist frets that she "gets away with it" and declares to the boys over their lunchtime martinis that, by God, he would soon put a stop to it if his wife developed any fancy ideas of a career. No female is about to deball him! That is his leit-motif, that the man married to a career woman must of necessity be less than a man. He cannot conceive of a male-female relationship in which both are willing to defy all convention so that their individual and unique gifts may be mutually realized. Because he cannot conceive of such a relationship, because he has never known the male and female as true helpmates in the most old- and yet new-fashioned sense, she has no redress.

It is in the realm of the sexual, however, that the black and the woman share the most vicious stereotyping. Both are depicted as essentially passive, sentient beings. They initiate nothing—but sex. For the myth that the woman and black are both secretly, helplessly carnal has as much hold over the male mind today as it ever had. This sexuality is the polarity of their passivity; one result of this is that it is viewed as disproportionately gross.

"A woman is capable of gratifying two or three vigorous men simultaneously without suffering in any way," wailed Schopenhauer seven centuries after the chastity belt was invented. Today the same mentality confides that "woman can do it twenty times a day if she likes." Like a pinpoint of pressure on his anger is the lively awareness of the male lack of control over the female in this area. Traditionally, woman in marriage has been part of the man's property, rather like the piano. Yet in this myth man faces the fact that she can rob him of his weapon and leave him a slave to his need for emotional excitement and psychological intimacy which she can fulfill "twenty times a day." In the slow boil of his mind woman and promiscuity ride hand in hand. She is Ida kneeling at Val's feet "gobbling it" in Henry Miller's *Sexus,* or Denise with her "angry tongue and voracious mouth going wild" in Norman Mailer's *The American Dream.* Or she is the frigid wife in Eldridge Cleaver's *Soul on Ice* being "turned on" with the purchase of a black man's "services."

The parallel of the myth of black sexuality and female sexuality is undeniable. While the body of the female is depicted as formless and soft—an extension of her mind—the body of the black is historically projected as a form of raw, brute force, a piece of machinery powered by the sweat of the brow. The black lives "naturally," being able to mate any time, any place and anywhere the spirit moves him. And according to this stereotype, it moves him all the time, like Schopenhauer's woman. And like the woman, the black does not live by rational decision; he is programmed to live by molecular drives. If woman's sexuality is seen as a threat, it is second only to the threat of the black man's penis. Like a million hidden Nikes they lie all over the North American continent ready to rise up and strike. We see a fine example of this mood when the late Frantz Fanon quotes Michel Cournot in *Black Skin, White Masks:*

When he has thrust it into your wife, she has really felt something. It is a revelation. In the chasm that it has left your little toy will be lost. Pump away until the room is awash with your sweat, you might as well be singing. This is goodbye. . . . Four Negroes with their penises exposed would fill a cathedral.

In this weird flight of fancy, the white male projects onto the Negro all the ferment of his own sexual agonies—particularly his deep concern about penis length and thickness, a widespread anxiety even among experienced men—and by making the black man an animal elevates his own humanity.

How do these attitudes relate to the deep bitterness that exists between the sexes? What is cause and what effect in the disastrous and antagonistic male-female relationships?

# VIII

When its members are finally counted, the American feminist liberation movement will probably split neatly into two camps, conservatives in one, radicals in the other. Although their theories and practices differ widely, ultimately both camps believe there is only one problem and that is the "man problem."

It is false to assume that all feminists are man-haters. It would be equally false to deny that the element which will ultimately hold both conservatives and radicals together in some loose form of alliance is an antagonism towards the male. The form that this antagonism assumes varies greatly from one feminist to another. The range is infinite, from that of amusement at male antics to that of an implacable hostility. The more radical the movement, the more radical the personal antagonism towards the male.

Where this radical antagonism exists it assumes the force of an overwhelming passion, but a passion so authentic that it appears to strike a responsive note in even the most conservative feminist, even if the response is limited to a theoretical acceptance. I have heard this hate disgorged at sensitivity sessions with a facility and raw relish that would turn men pale. For some feminists it is a thin edge removed from an expression in physical violence, the need for which is expressed by the number of women who now take lessons in karate, tai kwon do and judo. These activities give women an outlet for their anger, quite apart from a sense of bodily prowess, for this anger cannot find words grand enough for its dimensions. Women do not have the large vocabulary of derogatory terms for men that men have for women. Even the *nicest* man, a man whose mouth wouldn't melt butter in the presence of a woman, has a list of his own to speed communication with other men: woman is a broad, a pig, a dog, a bitch, slut, harpie, a good lay or a nice piece, and so on. The knowledge that these words are there ready within the male mind, even if rarely employed by some men, has an enraging effect on the female, conservative or radical. In one sense it paralyzes her; she can make no move in any direction without being awarded one of these labels. In her impotence she is thrust towards a violence that of necessity takes a bodily form. For what can a woman call a man, either aloud or within the privacy of her mind in a moment of extreme anger, but a weakling word like prick or son-of-a-bitch? Again, she is like a Negro who has been called nigger; to say honkey or whitey takes the skin off nobody's back or the edge off nobody's anger. Similarly, there is no verbal way in which a woman can fittingly return an insult from the arsenal of man's vocabulary.

Without the means of ventilating her feelings verbally,

and trapped within a construct that demands that all women be ladies to earn their sweets, the female's hostility towards the male has gone unheeded for centuries. Now that women are pushing themselves to their feet, the first stages of the movement are being characterized by the unleashing of a fury towards the male. This hatred for the male, and its traditional but now accelerated expression in sexual terms, is the most destructive influence within the woman's movement.

In its most extreme form this hate for man is expressed in articles such as those that suggest women skip sex for the duration of the struggle for liberation; if genital tensions exist while they are so struggling, however, they can masturbate. In its normal expression this hate assumes the aspect of an abrasive tone, stance, look, attitude, whenever a male appears on the horizon—it is as if the female body freezes. But I find myself asking if this freeze springs out of hate or out of fear? What have been the relationships and the sexual experiences of those who would advocate holding off for the duration and seeking a "satisfactory" outlet in masturbation? Masturbation and true sexual pleasure are as antithetical as God is to the devil. A woman who would view masturbation as an adequate substitute for coitus is a woman who sees herself a victim of the male, who sees herself in coitus only in terms of a debased sexual object, a woman who has never experienced enhancement by the sexual act but who, on the contrary, feels so degraded and so sacrificed that some form of compensation or recompense should be awarded her for the damage done.

It comes as no surprise that a well-read pamphlet in the movement is Ann Koedt's *The Myth of the Vaginal Or-*

*gasm*. It comes as no surprise because all sociological data garnered on the subject indicates that orgasm, vaginal or otherwise, is an unknown sexual experience for an unknown number of women. Why this vocation for sexual death?

We find ourselves back again and not inappropriately looking at the psychological mold into which the infant girl is squeezed. We see her by the time she is five moving in a hothouse which evolves around her body, and in this importance of her body lies her difference from the male. (It is no accident that many successful women such as Catherine Drinker Bowen and Marya Mannes, as well as the many lesser successful such as myself, were raised in the same atmosphere as their brothers.) In this atmosphere "femininity" assumes all the aspects of a vocation: it requires a scrupulous and guarded devotion, a serenity of mind, a delicacy of body. Any hint of the coarse or the natural should be eliminated. The unspoken emphasis in a constantly transmitted message is that woman's vocation is to lift man above his brute and animal nature.

With the passing of time the girl has no alternative but to perceive her body as a prize, a prize that goes to the man who manages to throw a ring around her. Into marriage she goes—or into an affair—with a clear image of her body as precious and unique, sensitive and in some misty way an expression of her soul. So she *gives* herself in intercourse; there has been nothing in her training to suggest that the man is giving just as much of his body and soul. The relationship from its inception is that of bodily giver and taker. The psychological ambiance of mutuality and reciprocity has no place in the traditional female perception of the sex act. That there is a wide spectrum of female reaction to intercourse is obvious. To some it is a terror, to some a joy, to millions it appears to this day as a sacrifice, a duty, a payment for the meal ticket of marriage. You might say that times have changed but all around is evidence that women continue to live within the near psychopathology imposed upon certain perceptions in their childhood: the radical male-hating feminists are the best example of this near psychopathology.

If there was nothing in the girl's training to suggest that sex should be a pleasant, reciprocal joy and a mutual giving not just of body but of psyche, there was much in her growing up to suggest that if it was not pleasant for her, it certainly was for him. And as orgasm comes easier for the male than the female, and as some pleasure is in fact guaranteed to the male by mere participation in the act, the image of the female as sexual benefactor is deeply entrenched in female psychology. It is an image that the courts acknowledge and adhere to when they order alimony paid to a healthy and youthful ex-wife who is perfectly capable of supporting herself. Instead of being grateful that she has at last gotten rid of the brute, she expects to be paid for having slept with him.

All this ties in with the image of sex as degrading. All the training of the girl child has been to drive off threatening influences, to preserve her ladylike role at all costs. Nothing has prepared her to accept the violence, the heat, the sweat and the total tumult of coupling, with authentic pleasure. To abandon herself to a spontaneous enjoyment of sex, a spontaneous acceptance of the other, would require the utmost assertion of her own individuality and an almost total destruction of all the old former values. So it is, as Simone de Beauvoir remarked, that it is many a husband who prepares his wife unwittingly for another man. Unlike man, woman does not marry for sex. Woman marries to fulfill the image that has been superimposed on her, the image of the successful executive's wife, or the mother fulfilling God's plan or whatever the pretty fiction is, all sitting in a glossy house where there is no work to be done yet never a pillow out of place.

Yet what she gets is sex, dirty sex night and day, and she gets it in the context of a society where sex comes on like a pollutant spewed out by industry. Its image is in the swollen breasts of the *Playboy* bunny, or more so in her little erected tail, or in the full center spreads of the nude magazines, in the sprays to deodorize the body, in the beauty contests where like cows in the stockyard the contestants offer their buttocks and breasts for male evaluation. Sex comes in dirty jokes and double entendres and in a flood of symbolism out of the drugstores and out of the television sets and out of every magazine and movie. The tragedy of the sexually uninterested woman is that all this cheap commercial fiction, which is as alien to real sex as romantic courtship is to marriage, is the model from which she derives the meaning of her sexuality. She perceives herself as a sexual object and this awareness, which reaches its peak within the marital bed, leaves her empty, repulsed and angry.

Woman's capacity to blossom and respond sexually is based almost solely on her evaluation of herself. If she believes that she is a worthwhile human being, a person different but equal in all ways with her partner, she can find in sex a glorious affirmation and enhancement of her own value.

But if the woman feels she is of little value, that her thoughts, her feelings, perceptions and ambitions are inferior, and if in fact her exposure to life has provided one consistent affirmation of this image—then she will not perceive herself as an equal with some command and control in an act of mutual joy. She will perceive herself as an inferior, as the sexual object of all her social conditioning, and in turn will experience a sense of degradation. Beneath her sexual passivity is a desire to punish the male for his pleasure, for to the woman who has been thwarted and blocked, robbed of her ambitions, who has had her visions ignored, her legitimate aspirations scorned, the sex act assumes the aspects of all her former submissions—to parents, to family, church, father confessor, professor, to the whole system. There is no possibility of her acting in an honest, spontaneous and authentic manner. She has spent her life denying her honesty, spontaneity and authenticity. Why should the patterns of a lifetime's training drop from her merely because she steps into bed with a male? The idea that there should be a reciprocal exchange of sexual activity and pleasure is a fiction because she has experienced no true reciprocity on any other level of life.

When I say that the female who is passive wishes to punish her man for his pleasure, it is not to deny the bitter tears of many women who, now used, are abandoned by the satiated male. The desire to punish need not be conscious; in fact it can be in one sense a perfect form of reciprocity. The husband who consistently has to face an uninterested and passive wife has two alternatives and it costs him whichever one he chooses. He can open himself to further hurt and humiliation by facing and attempting to improve the situation; or he can take his pleasure, close his mind to her state, and so justify her passivity. She wins either way.

I am stating that women who do not enjoy sex—more specifically those who appear incapable of vaginal orgasm —are victims of a system which has systematically divorced them from any form of spontaneous, creative activity and that this process of divorce from reality has been exacerbated by presenting sex as a conflict between the base and the desirable. Further, in the sexual act the man can represent, to a creative or naturally exploratory woman, all the forces of her childhood oppression. The touch of his hand on her breasts, hips or vagina, can produce a sweep of hate; and all the changing of positions, the love play, the stimulation of erogenic areas, and all the desire for orgasm and tenderness of the male cannot release the reflexes locked away in childhood. Nor can his or her yearnings eradicate the impression gained by the child from the wider world— the clear impression of woman as a sexual object. This brings us to another factor in this complex problem.

As an object the female body has had an historic double function. As we discussed earlier, it not only perpetuated the species but at the same time provided the prime outlet for male sexual drives. The reproductive role of the female body is now obsolete, the sexual role is not.

If we look at two women who are using a totally safe contraceptive, we find a direct relationship between the sexual role, the use of the contraceptive and the ground swell of hate towards the male as we see it expressed by some cells of the movement. One of these two women enjoys sex; even at those times when her chemistry runs naturally tepid, intercourse deepens her sense of pleasurable serenity and enhances her feelings of dignity and worth. At the pit of her consciousness is a clear awareness that the sex act fulfills no societal function. It puts no more hands to the fields, no more backs to the crops, furnishes no more raw labor for industry and no more warriors for war. Sexual intercourse for her has meaning only to the extent that it satisfies her or her lover's physiological or psychological needs, or, more happily, a combination of both their needs. For centuries, this woman has been programmed like all women to reproduce through this act. By taking a contraceptive, she precludes such a possibility, yet the satisfactions of being a loved and desired object which such intimacies arouse take absolute precedence over her historic programming.

But what of the woman who has never experienced spontaneous, authentic sexual need, the woman who goes through life sincerely believing that lust is alien to the nature of the female? By going to a doctor, taking a prescription to the drug store, getting a Dial-Pak, putting a pill into the mouth every night or morning, the frigid woman aids and abets an act which, for whatever the reason, she loathes, an act which in her perception debases her. And so an already miserable sexual situation is charged with a hopeless contradiction. Hopeless, not only because of the woman's daily and voluntary preparation but because the sole purpose of that preparation is to remove all societal consequence from the act and contain its meaning within the bodies of the two parties concerned.

It takes no particular talent to see that now that the sex act fulfills no societal function it has become critical that sexual intercourse express or engender authentic communication. As we discussed, there are many ways of precluding this possibility. One way of guaranteeing there will be no real communication is to define the other in one context only, to view the other under a label, a word, a title. The question springs out: how does society define woman? And the answer springs back: in a biological context, as it has for centuries. So this is what we face. With absolutely safe contraception, with an exploding new awareness that way out there nothing is as rigid or as absolute as we had thought it to be, with a whole society slap up against the question of its own nature and all the institutions that are projections of that nature, the male-female sex act could become a true sacrament. It could be for all what it is now only for some—*two souls on a trip towards the ground of being.* Yet there is no possibility of this while society insists on continuing to define woman within a biological context. No matter what avenue we journey up in our discussions, this is the conclusion that awaits us. For the very environment that supported this generic role has been destroyed and man realizes this at some level and in his desperation to avoid change and hang on to his beloved and secure constructs of the female he makes a sick ado about the female body, blowing up the breasts with silicone so that she might be more readily identified in the old, familiar terms.

Yet all the avoidance mechanisms of the male will not change reality. *The reality is that society has reached a point where woman must be redefined totally apart from her biological function.* She has lost the only role that was socially imperative and now starts out, at the end of the twentieth century, on a long and painful route of repro-gramming.

Yet if it is true that there is no possibility that the male-female relationship can become a true sacrament as long as society defines woman within a biological context, there is also no possibility if the female continues to blame the male for every frustration she suffers as a woman. To use hate as a working philosophy can only draw energies and attention away from real liberation.

# CHAPTER

# IX

It is an oft-repeated axiom in the movement that half the people in the world are women. So it follows that half the people in the world are men. As the ultimate end of every revolution should be to enrich the quality of life, again it follows that sane minds have no alternative but to move forward in the direction of a more humanized future. Such a future remains in the realm of the impossible while half of the population holds the other half responsible for its every abuse. If we have learned anything in the last twenty-five years it is that those who live with their hatred today are the material for the storm troopers of tomorrow, for the characteristic that is common to all who hate is not the desire to mend society but to destroy it.

The unstated essence of this hate for the male is hatred for those institutions which he has created to control and psychically starve woman into a permanent state of subservience.

Yet if men cannot understand the female agony, their

115

blindness is no less destructive than the inability of antagonistic women to grasp the realities of the male world in
which they struggle to succeed. Ironically it is often the ignorance of the woman or her stubborn insistence on clinging to romantic notions that brings her marriage to ruin.

Let us start with the myth of the millenium—which is
that all American male adults like and want children. The
male is as supreme an example as is the female of a product
of two different value systems. He develops within a society
that classifies him as something less than a fulfilled man unless he produces offspring. Once he produces these children, he often finds they cannot be fitted anywhere into the
mode of modern life. It is more than probable that the urge
to reproduce is still as strong in the marrow of a European's bones as it was a century ago. But the American has
had every one of his basic values challenged by the mere
existential realities of modern urban American life. Moral-
ists are ever ready to blast modern man for his selfish, he-
donistic attitudes but the circumstances of his life are such
that there is simply no time for him to be a father. This is
particularly the case where the male practices the ethics of
our affluent society—that he be ambitious, aggressive, ca-
reer-minded, dedicated to his work, willing to uproot the
family time and time again to move another niche up the
ladder of success. If he is at home and not away on one of
his endless trips, he leaves that home at seven A.M., enters a
dog-eat-dog world and returns twelve hours later wrung
out. If his wife is an ambitious woman—ambitious not cre-
atively but ambitious to acquire an image of affluence and
success—and if she demands that her mate father some
children, the responsibility for creating intolerable pressures

is hers. She has demanded the right to have children, then deprived him through her image-seeking of the freedom to be a true father.

Not the least of the reasons why the American male is losing the desire for children is the contingent loss of spontaneous privacy with his mate. Women do not appear to understand this basic need of men, but if there is one element that kills romance, and can eventually kill a marriage, it is this loss. As woman's inability to react spontaneously precludes her sexual fulfillment, so does the lack of spontaneous privacy preclude the sexual fulfillment of men. Spontaneity is the most essential of all the ingredients that make for good sex. Without it, there can be no psychological intimacy and the sex act becomes a dead ritual of no more importance than blowing one's nose. I said earlier that many women are not aware of the male's need for spontaneous expression but perhaps it is not, after all, an unawareness. It could well be a desire to punish, a confusion of animality with spontaneity. I have found, working almost exclusively with men for twenty years, that they do not as a rule discuss sex. Despite talk to the contrary, the subject of their own sexual behavior and that of their mates is very much a private matter. But men do talk about their need for privacy. On the West Coast, and perhaps it is the same on the East, male office workers have even coined a term for the man who is fortunate enough to be able to go home daily for lunch—a "nooner." I have no doubt this will raise the hackles of anger among women who hate and fear men, for what they hate is not so much man but humanity in general. They loathe the nature of man and refuse to face the fact that it was God and not General Motors who created man and all his drives. They long for the world to be some other way, for man to be something other than what he is, failing to realize that only if the realities of man's weaknesses and strengths are embraced can woman realize herself.

If we return to the fact that spontaneous privacy with one's mate is precluded by modern life, and that this ingredient is critical to a growing relationship, we see this preclusion as a disastrous loss of freedom, a loss springing from two sources—the male's place of employment and the presence of his children. It is commonplace to hear women say: "Bob and I have never quarreled over a thing in our lives except the children." Or: "I don't know whether Charlie is typical or not but he told me last night that he can hardly wait until the kids grow up and leave home." Charlie is typical of an unknown number of men pressured into having children by their own self-image and the insistence of wives and mothers-in-law. For the wife, children were necessary to turn the house into a home. For the mother-in-law, grandchildren were necessary for a meaningful existence. But for the vast majority of American males in the year 1970, the painful truth is that children are an economic burden, a challenge, demand time he does not have, precipitate states of anxiety and become the primary impediment to his spontaneity as a man with his mate. All this combines to make fatherhood a state he would willingly forgo.

If woman has been programmed to bear, man has been programmed just as long to hunt and fight. Through the centuries the male mind and body have been engaged in a constant battle with the natural forces—with the weather, finding a way through the woods, ploughing, taking care of the horses, forging rivers. A sensitivity to the physical realities of this world has been programmed into the male genes. But how does the poor eviscerated bull now spend his days but shuffling paper in some vast concrete mausoleum, the sounds of the rivers and the birds and the thrills and joys of the hunt lost to him forever. The body is not so easily ignored: the phenomena of recurrent depression that is as commonplace a complaint today as a headache might well have its genesis in the body living a life that, according to its programming, is flaccid to the point of insanity.

One of the basic needs expressed by feminists is for fulfilling and creative work and the validity of this need is too obvious to be denied. Yet isn't it a fact that the armies of men presently deployed in the world of business spend their lives doing work that is distinguished from housework in its creative possibilities only by the ride into the office and the coffee break? Admittedly, the ride and the break, and the possibilities of seeing something such as a traffic accident, or running into an old friend are stimuli that the housewife does not have. They are perhaps sufficient to keep the man in touch with reality, sufficient to keep him from going insane. There is another kind of stimulus, too, that should be taken into account, one that goes unappreciated in the female world.

Men, in their business or craft or in the armed services, are subject to a type of criticism that women do not experience. In this society a man's work is an integral part of his manhood and consequently any attack on his ability is an attack on that manhood. A working woman in this society is still viewed primarily as a woman. She might err as a stenographer but she can still be a successful woman in society's eyes, as a mother, housewife, cook, etc. Criticism directed at the female's work capacity in no way impinges on her value as a woman. But it digs deep into a man's sense of his own manhood. Further, the male is subject to public criticism. There is nothing comparable in the housewife's life; in fact, woman is not expected to make any substantial advance in her skills. It is as if all possible growth is frozen in her twenties. Her housework is not subjected to critical inspection nor are her housekeeping skills assessed by two or three superiors. But if a man does not receive a promotion or wage increase, if the assessment of his labors is not favorable, there is a clear inference he does not have what it takes and he is publicly labeled as a failure. Society will then extend to his mate a certain sympathy—providing she does not love her man too enthusiastically. For nothing offends society more than the woman who loves, respects and lauds a man whom the world perceives as a failure. In the current ethos the female pursues and loves the successful man; there is no place in this ethos for the guy who hasn't got it to be loved. According to this ethos it is money, success and title that engender love; for a woman to love a man who does not have these attributes, no matter what his real value *as a man,* is to fly in the face of the mythology that is currently holding the world of business together.

None of the above is an attempt to share sweets or lay blame, but is merely a passing effort to bring some of the realities of the male world into focus. What emerges is the recognition that, although early man had the opportunity to be the architect of our institutions and choose for himself a favored position within them, today these institutions are victimizing the male almost as much as they are the female.

You might well ask why women should sensitize them-selves to this fact when men remain so blind or indifferent to the realities of the woman's world. In any therapy there must be a shifting of stance or emphasis of viewpoint. Such a shift is well on its way to being forced upon the male whether he wants it or not. If woman makes a parallel attempt then history might well be accelerated to the good.

We said earlier that a psychological intimacy is a prereq-uisite for successful sex. And the question arises: how is this intimacy possible in view of the female's lack of spontaneity and the debased image of sex in our society? To answer it, we have to start with the notion that a male and female confronting one another are caught by such a series of mys-teries, move on such a circuit of mysteries, that the sum total of their sense of interest and puzzlement locks to form an intimacy that escapes all categorization. In common parlance they are "in love." This love is an encounter with the reality of the other, a total openness and awareness of the other's being, the other's presence, the other's *now*. The nature of this experience is such that cultural superimposi-tions begin to appear in their true perspective. Sex as duty, man as oppressor, spontaneity as unladylike—all these im-ages recede before the reality of a total and mutual accep-tance of the other. As we have discussed, there can be no acceptance without some insight into the existential realities of the other's life. Once this insight is integrated into the re-lationship, the path is clear not only for a joyous sex life but for the extraordinary phenomenon of the vaginal or-gasm. If the vaginal orgasm is widely believed to be a myth it is because it *is* a myth for all but very few women.

It was not until reading *The Second Sex* that I learned there was a question as to its existence. When I found that De Beauvoir doubted its existence, I started to doubt De Beauvoir: those trips between Paris and New York appeared dull, a chase rather than a capture.

The pamphlet, *The Myth of the Vaginal Orgasm,* provides a perfect illustration of why the vaginal orgasm is a myth to so many women. It describes the clitoris, quoting G. Lombard Kelly in *Sexual Feeling in Married Men and Women:*

> The head of the clitoris is also composed of erectile tissue, and it possesses a very sensitive epithelium or surface covering, supplied with special nerve endings called genital corpuscles, which are peculiarly adapted for sensory stimulation that under proper mental conditions terminates in the sexual orgasm. No other part of the female generative tract has such corpuscles.

Kinsey's *Sexual Behavior in the Human Female* provides the description of the vagina, which is:

> like nearly all other internal body structures, poorly supplied with end organs of touch. The internal entodermal origin of the lining of the vagina makes it similar in this respect to the rectum and other parts of the digestive tract.

The conclusion drawn is that arousal and consequent satisfaction can be achieved only by stimulation of the clitoris. Therefore, the vaginal orgasm does not exist. But there is yet a further conclusion and it is this conclusion that reveals the hidden thrust behind Ann Koedt's pamphlet:

Men fear that they will become sexually expendable if the clitoris is substituted for the vagina as a center of pleasure for women. Actually this has a great deal of validity if one considers *only* the anatomy. [Italics hers.] The position of penis inside the vagina, while perfect for reproduction, does not necessarily stimulate an orgasm in women because the clitoris is located externally and higher up. Women must rely upon indirect stimulation in the "normal" position.

*Lesbian sexuality could make an excellent case, based upon anatomical data, for the extinction of the male organ. Albert Ellis says something to the effect that a man without a penis can make a woman an excellent lover.* [Italics mine.]

Considering that the vagina is very desirable from a man's point of view, purely on physical grounds, one begins to see the dilemma for men. . . . Aside from the strictly anatomical reasons why women might equally seek other women as lovers, there is a fear on men's part that women will seek the company of other women on a full, human basis. The establishment of clitoral orgasm as fact would threaten the heterosexual *institution*. [Italics hers.]

In other words, a lesbian relationship is posited as being as natural and perhaps even more sexually satisfying than a love relationship can ever be between man and woman. This may be the case for a limited number of women who have an abnormal hormonal or psychological background, but to suggest that this type of relationship is a desirable norm for the majority of women is grossly pathological. The pamphlet glosses over the central fact of good orgasm —*that sex is largely in the head.*

Aside from the above mentioned direct and indirect stimulations of the clitoris, there is a third way an orgasm may be triggered. This is through mental (cortical) stimulation, where the imagination stimulates the brain, which in turn stimulates the genital corpuscles of the glands to set off an orgasm. (*The Myth of the Vaginal Orgasm*)

Examples that illustrate that sex is largely a matter of the mind are to be found wherever one looks. One woman might be "frigid" with her husband but achieves orgasm effortlessly with a lover whose physical attributes and modus operandi are the same or even less potent than those of the husband. It is a common experience of many marriages that the enjoyment derived from sex varies greatly and that the excitement and pleasure derived, and the intensity of orgasm achieved, has far more to do with the state of mind of the participants than the foreplay or act itself. A warm, romantic movie, a sexy book, a fight, even a bereavement or loss, or just a sudden insight into the depths of the other's yearnings—in fact almost any shift or change in the day-to-day emotional diet can predispose a loving couple to good orgasm. *The element that precludes good orgasm is the nonacceptance, for whatever the reason, of the partner.* It is many a wife who knows she cannot arouse her husband no matter how intense the degree of stimulation she might use if he is genuinely angry, hurt or humiliated. If good sex is merely a matter of physical stimulation why won't his penis stiffen and erect on demand? For the same reason she cannot "come" if she has taken into her bed a mental bagful of resentment against her mate. As we discussed earlier, her image of sex is already highly charged with ambivalence; unless she can forgive her mate all his faults within the privacy of her own heart, and embrace him in his totality, she will never achieve a vaginal orgasm.

To attempt to describe the vaginal orgasm is to run the risk of being charged with offering a simplistic testimonial as a substitute for verified fact. Yet there is no alternative, for it is more than likely that the vaginal orgasm will never be verified by the cathodes and wires of the sex research laboratories; possibly it will never come to life in the abstract and dehumanized setting of a sex research laboratory. There is no room in it for a trace of falsity or of usage. It touches being; it is not for sale or examination nor would it turn itself over for an accounting by those who would attempt to capture its essence in formulas and numbers.

The vaginal orgasm is a total neurological, physiological and psychological experience. The term *vaginal* is misleading for there is an orgasm of a seemingly identical nature and intensity experienced by the male. That this orgasm is experienced by the male apparently only at those times that it is experienced by the female tends to support my belief that the vaginal orgasm is a total exterior expression of the deepest interior intimacy. That is, a meeting and mingling of two loving human souls very close to the ground of being. Clitoral orgasm bears only a puny resemblance to the force and fulfillment of vaginal orgasm. Clitoral orgasm and its physical reactions are confined mainly to the vaginal area, the breasts, the hips and buttocks and perhaps the legs. The vaginal orgasm sweeps the entire body in wave after wave from the tips of the fingers to the top of the head to the tips of the toes and all that is in between. So it is with the male who has experienced this phenomenon. He will describe normal orgasm as just a shadow, a neurological or masturbatory type experience—an experience perhaps best de-

scribed as a head-of-the-dick orgasm as compared to the totality of the male "vaginal" orgasm.

The use of the word *vaginal* now becomes patently
unacceptable. As it is experienced by both male and female, I shall refer to it from now on as the "total" orgasm.

One characteristic of the total orgasm that has significance is the physiological state that lingers for some time
following. It is a state of total relaxation, a state that, as far
as mental activity is concerned, might well parallel the
alpha waves of a Hindu meditator. This is significant: in
the *Journal of the American Psychoanalytic Association* for
July, 1968, Dr. Mary J. Sherfey remarks that, on the basis
of the Masters-Johnson *Human Sexual Response* research,
"to all intents and purposes, the human female is sexually
insatiable in the presence of the highest degree of sexual sa-
tiation."

Is it not a clear possibility that this "insatiability" reflects
effort rather than achievement, a reaching out and seeking
rather than a taking-in and finding? If we look at the
women *used*—and *used* is the best possible word to describe what was done to them—we find an extraordinary
situation. Masters and Johnson used what they euphemisti-
cally call "female surrogates" to service the forty-one single
men who were accepted by the foundation for treatment.
These thirteen women *volunteered* for the experiment—to
have sexual intercourse with an unknown number of strangers while being observed and photographed—*and were en-
joined against becoming emotionally involved with any of
their partners.* Four of the women had already been divorced and sexual unhappiness was a key factor in their di-
vorces. Conclusions regarding the sexual behavior and re-

actions of *all women* have been drawn from the behavior of these thirteen unpaid prostitutes. One of the conclusions is mentioned above—that women are sexually insatiable—and the second is that there is no physiological difference between a clitoral orgasm or a vaginal orgasm. How on earth do Masters and Johnson know? What a crock! If the Masters-Johnson findings indicate anything it is that a woman with a low and inferior self-image (as these women surely had) experiences overwhelming difficulty in achieving a full orgasm. Full, good orgasm not only requires a sense of enhancement but also, as we discussed earlier, an authentic psychological intimacy. If these women acted as if they were insatiable, even following clitoral orgasm, it is simply because the real fire of total orgasm had not been quenched.

I am suggesting that clitoral orgasm is a peripheral sexual response, a puny neurological relief that can never satisfy the craving for psychological intimacy, the disposition towards and the need for which plays a large part in the initiation of the sex act. The nature of true sexuality involves the freest, purest and most authentic forces of mind, body and soul. If this combination is present, coupled with a total awareness of and openness to the Other, the act of sexual intercourse can transcend all fleshly meaning. This is the essential meaning of coitus that no laboratory can subject to its scrutiny; its very existence defies proof.

The mystery of the total orgasm touches on this element of transcendence. Of flesh, there could be nothing more fleshly, of sweat nothing more sweaty, of movement nothing more violent. Yet the sum total of those prolonged waves adds up to the antithesis of all that is of the flesh and there is a sure knowledge that one has come near, if not touched, the ground of being. That the total orgasm is experienced by few women is a fact of experience; it stands in one sense as a mystery but never as a myth. As to the reasons why it is experienced so seldom, the answer lies in the twisted complexities of one single fact—humanity still has not learned the art of loving.

My use of the word *love* and the insistence on psychological intimacy will be rejected by some, such as the Kinsey and Masters-Johnson researchers. They will claim many men and woman experience highly satisfactory sexual relations where there is neither love nor psychological intimacy involved, where the coupling has been an act of impulse with a near-total stranger met two hours earlier at a cocktail party. Good orgasm, they will say, has nothing whatsoever to do with love.

Of course it is possible to achieve a satisfactory sexual experience with a stranger; life and literature are full of such incidences. Such a couple, removed from all sense of responsibility and engaged in a taboo and erotic act, experience many emotions, primarily a mutual recognition of the other's lust and a willingness to serve it. This acknowledged recognition in such a taboo area could constitute a form of psychological intimacy, sufficient for a neurological and physiological release of tension. They can achieve the Big O, as *Esquire* so neatly labels it. But orgasm is not the sole aim of intercourse; it is in one sense part of a deeper intercourse that, exhibiting itself in feelings of tenderness and joy, can precede and trail after the actual act for hours. There is none of this psychological harvest in the one-night stand; if engaged in often enough, sex of this type corrodes one's view of oneself and of the entire world. Unlike the psychological intimacy that springs from an acknowledgment of the other's totality, intimacy that is based solely on the need to rid oneself of sexual tension diminishes, rather than enhances, one's self-image. And in so doing reduces one's capacity to engage in an enduring and creative relationship with another.

As the word *love* means different things to different people, so does the word *sex*. There are a variety of love relationships and a variety of sex relationships. What then makes the total orgasm so important? What difference does it make whether it is achieved or not? The question that should be asked is not whether the total orgasm is important but whether reality is important.

Within the animal world, within all of creation, the primary drive is a coming together of the sexes. This coming together of the sexes is a reality. Have we reached the point where all our sexual, social, economic and political constructs are more important than reality, where we prefer to choose fiction, where we attempt to play God by living through our images rather than experiencing the reality of the creation around us?

How does this relate to all the subjects previously discussed—male-female antagonism, the male world, the orgasm, the liberation movement?

The individual who knows what reality is suffers no disturbance and no competition from social constructs. There is a force in reality that is devastating. There is a meaning, beauty, and an experience in reality that far surpasses the force of these constructs. If woman is going to be fulfilled, if she is going to experience the inherent forces that have molded her through the entire process of evolution, it can only be at the expense of these social institutions that have deprived her of reality. *The total orgasm is the reality of her existence as a woman.* All the dirty diapers, the new curtains, whether Joe gets a promotion, whether the new car should be a sedan or a station wagon, whether one's hair should be dyed red, black or brown—all these mind-polluting, soul-destroying questions wither in the face of reality. If woman can experience reality—and I suggest that the total orgasm is the most natural and fruitful route— then she can be free for the first time from the piddling and dehumanizing forces that have robbed her of any meaning-ful existence. Absolutely, this does not mean that orgasm is the solution of the female problem; this would posit a clear absurdity. It is a part, and far from the whole, of her life. It is part of a life that might or might not involve marriage, children, housework or a career. We understand well the consequences to the mind and body of a poor, inadequate diet; why must we insist on denying the consequences of other instinctive bodily needs merely because they do not reveal themselves immediately in clear-cut terms?

I am saying that there is a real existence that turns our vanities into straw and that this existence depends largely on the degree in which we become one with the forces of reality. A major aspect of this process of becoming one with reality lies in finding fulfillment in the dynamic force of life as it is expressed in the coming together of the sexes.

# CHAPTER

# X

Hard evidence about the inner dynamics of the so-called "normal" marriage is scarce, but that dramatic changes are occurring within marriage is evident from the widespread and open discussions on premarital and extramarital affairs, the increasing number of women in the labor force, the easy social acceptance of divorce and the widening of grounds for divorce in practically every state.

The feminists are in no way the initiators of this revolution within marriage; the revolution was under way decades before the modern feminists came into existence. However, they do provide a visible and organized body through which society can vent its deep marital woes. Further, in their own examination and persistent demands for an overhauling of the traditional marital institution, the feminists are currently providing the single most powerful antitraditional thrust. This alone should guarantee the feminists a high place in heaven, not to mention a lot of supporters on earth, for possibly more cruelty has been perpetuated in the name of marriage than in the name of religion.

Modern marriage is a treasury of myth and superstition. Millions who scorn religious faith as being an opiate and a denial of reason seize and in turn are captivated by the mythology of romantic love and marriage. It is commonly believed, for instance, that men and women marry by choice; but the male has no more choice than the female as to his ultimate domestic destiny. That all "normal" people marry is a basic premise of Western social thought. We have touched at length on the domestication of the girl and the fact that marriage is presented to her as the only goal worthy of a "real" woman. The fact is that the male is under a similar, if somewhat less intense, pressure. His marriage, too, is assumed from childhood. If he does not marry by the time he is in his late twenties, he will be suspected of homosexuality, or held to be in need of some form of counseling or psychological assistance.

If a man is ambitious, he must marry or face the very real possibility of severe handicapping in his advancements. Management sensitivity to the existence of, and mileage to be extracted from, the executive's wife is illustrated in this assessment of "Executive Wives," *California Management Review,* Spring, 1965.

> Even those couples who have established the wife's role in assisting her husband's career must redefine this role as each new promotion brings with it new demands on the wife and family and adjustments in personal relationships for all.
>
> Personnel executives, consulting psychologists, and executive recruiters cite these wifely drawbacks: prone to drinking too much; domineering, poorly informed; mentally un-

derdeveloped compared to her husband; resentful towards
the company for taking away her husband or forgetting her;
*excessive interest in her own career or activities, either so-
cial or business, to the detriment of her husband's.* [Italics
mine.]

The possible advantages to the company of a wives' program are enormous. A high degree of communication between company, employee and his family is fostered. The
morale of husband and wife would be aided, therefore im-
proving *the effectiveness of the manager.* [Italics mine.]

There is no hint that such a ruthless manipulation of the
marital bonds could invite pathological consequences (perhaps if there is any chance of a "possible advantage to the
company" it doesn't matter).

This quotation provides a sterling example of the many
roles which modern marriage is called upon to fill. The ambitious couple must burden themselves with a home, for instance: whether they need it, want it or can afford it is be-
side the point. Owning one's own home is necessary for the
image of permanency and stability which society demands.
Home ownership also provides the corporation with an easy
acid test of loyalty when the newly settled employee is
asked to now move elsewhere. In such a milieu, the house
is not a home but a backdrop, a stage scattered with all the
props necessary for the projection of a suitable "success"
image. As a man advances within the corporate system, the
house can become a power plant of imagery, reaching its
optimum potential as a stage in what is perhaps America's
greatest exercise in oneupmanship—the entertainment of
friends and associates.

When there is a house, there next must be children, for in

the mythology of business a man's ability to impregnate his wife is closely associated with his virility and creativity. The male's corporate image of uprighteousness and dedication is mystically but closely related to his ability to raise a family. Likewise the success of marriage and parenthood for both man and wife will depend, in the eyes of society, on whether or not the children surpass their parents. The rat race is not only for adults; the little rats must run faster too. Either that, or cope with a thousand subtle and punishing pressures. For although society is ostensibly child-centered it is in reality parent-centered. The myth is that marriage and parenthood exist for the sake of the children—the fact is that children usually exist for the sake of the parents. In the idealization of marriage, children now play an integral role, much of it false and often directly responsible for the untenable stresses that exist within the nuclear unit. In summary I am saying that there are an unknown number of men and women who would have been perfectly fulfilled in a single state but married because of psychological pressures; once they were married, they bent still further to social psychological pressures and reproduced a family. Then, because a couple's whole status, prestige and success are often intimately linked through the corporate structure to the success of that family, dissolution of the marriage involves dissolution or radical restructuring of every aspect of one's personal and business life—a prospect which few people have the courage, the energy or the money to face.

Perhaps the most destructive element in marriage as we have known it is the loving of only one member of the opposite sex. The exclusion of all other loves of the opposite sex is a patent absurdity; it runs counter to all of human nature. Human beings were meant to love. I am not speaking of sexual affairs although it would be to close one's eyes to reality to deny that some form of sexual expression might not be an incidental part of the larger picture. We are so terrified that this taboo gesture may be expressed, so frightened of ourselves and distrustful of our own goodness, that we cling to one man or one woman rather than expose ourselves to the misunderstandings and hurts that are almost inevitably involved in the development of a truly meaningful friendship. We have become so sex-oriented that a lively interest in and natural empathy with a member of the opposite sex is almost totally forbidden us. In fact we are allowed to have an affair before society will allow us to have a friendship. There is no reason why a woman cannot meet a man downtown for lunch or have him into her home for coffee and conversation; there is no reason why a man cannot do the same without the crippling and intimidating realization that society regards any such friendship in a degrading and demeaning light. Small wonder that so many married women are fossilized at thirty; five years have passed since they spoke to any man other than their husband, obstetrician or the butcher. They are not allowed by social tradition to speak to or make friends with half the population. Their husbands are only a little freer to develop friendships; affairs, however, are more accessible.

It should be clear I am not advocating affairs. In principle, it is basically dumb for a married woman to have an affair; she exposes herself, her spouse and her lover to a potentially terrible wound. Despite *Cosmopolitan*'s trumpeting of the delights of an affair, the realities can be totally dif-

ferent. Loving and good adults can be destroyed, children
can be made parentless, homes and hearts broken in what
can end up as a sordid and public mess. And the guilt that
is an integral part of an affair stands not only as an obsta-
cle to marital reconciliation but appears to precipitate hasty
remarriages which are no better than the original, both parties merely having hauled their unresolved problems from
one partner to the next.

Though extramarital affairs are and possibly always will
be socially and morally unacceptable, the fact remains that
falling in love, and sometimes passionately, with somebody
other than one's own spouse appears to be part of the
human condition. Undeniably such an affair can be a fan-
tastic growth experience. Whether this love is expressed sexually, or to what degree sexually, is a complex and individual matter and almost irrelevant to the central issue. For
the woman who married young and inexperienced in the
whole realm of interpersonal relationships, the experience
of a reciprocal love with another man can precipitate her into new depths of understanding, not only of herself but of
all men and women. If she is a responsible person and can
transfer this new knowledge into her own marriage then an
adulterous liaison can bring new life into a sagging relationship. If she uses her experience with another as a
weapon, it will destroy a marriage that probably should
have been dissolved in any case.

Marriage as we know it has survived because it is an arrangement suitable to our Western culture for the care and
raising of children. In former times the wife died after having the third or fourth child. The husband had the opportunity to marry several times; she was on the earth scarcely

long enough to ask what it was all about. Now couples are living together into their seventies and eighties. Yet we still believe that, with three and a half billion people on the face of the earth, a one-minute ceremony should limit our lives to a loving relationship with only one person.

Let me say again I am not advocating adultery. The human hurt and possible destruction in adultery are too real and too gross to be brushed aside. Yet I believe our reactions to adultery are extravagant and exaggerated. I am not speaking of persistent adultery or a lengthy affair, which would indicate that no true marriage was in existence in any case and the quicker it were dissolved the better. I am speaking of the act that one would normally call "out of character," the act that results from unbearable loneliness or fear or lust or love. From a moral viewpoint such an act is no worse than the acts of greed, injustice and inhumanity that are practiced publicly daily as an integral part of our capitalist system. Yet the traditional marriage, which forbids married persons to diffuse their emotional and affectional needs through healthy, nonadulterous friendships, is shattered when the hunger for friendship drives a party into adultery.

Whatever might be the risks involved, new forms and freedoms in male and female friendships will prove to be far less damaging than the patently absurd notion that once a man and woman marry they are then solely responsible for meeting and fulfilling one another's total emotional and intellectual needs. It is this philosophy that leaves the lonely married person with no alternative outlet other than adultery.

One of the most common remarks that the newly divorced make is that they are at last free to do things—go to symphony concerts, to movies, baseball, water skiing, or to learn new skills and crafts, change their hair style or entire life style. It is implied that such activities were not possible during the now-dissolved marriage. Yet on inquiry it appears that these activities were not only just as accessible, but that the other partner encouraged his or her spouse to engage in them. The other partner, too, had his or her dreams about getting up and out and doing things—of "really living." But both were paralyzed by the marriage. There are two elements at work here, both destructive and both an integral part of the mythology that surrounds the traditional marriage. One element we have just touched on —the unquestioned assumption in the face of all the counter evidence that when a man and woman marry they will meet all one another's emotional and intellectual needs. There is a second element, the negative side of the same coin. If a man and woman do not meet the totality of the other's needs—and who does or who can—engaging in activities and relationships without one's spouse is tantamount to a public admission of "difference"; it flies in the face of cherished "togetherness." Man and wife should be "one in flesh" and this concept is so deeply ingrained in our Western society as to preclude separate outings, let alone outings with members of the opposite sex.

Women are far more prone to victimize themselves within marriage than men; sacrifice is love and love is service. Men can scarcely be blamed for wondering whether such dedication to one's own demise as a human being is not a rather cunning psychological game, which of course it is, but it is a game women have been programmed into since childhood and therefore can scarcely help themselves from playing. Let us take the simple case of a woman who is interested in classical music. She enjoys symphony concerts; they bore him. He encourages her to go and, unable to understand her refusal, gives up in bewilderment or exasperation. She is being a martyr again! The realities are somewhat different. Few men realize the depths of a woman's feelings of inferiority. (They never stop to ask why every woman must think her body the most desirable of all bodies; they never stop to think that this body is the only thing a woman has.) Nor do men realize the feelings of inadequacy that thread their way through everything a woman does outside the realm of housekeeping. Woman has been trained to focus her life within the home; nothing in her training has suggested she develop lifelong nondomestic interests whose sole purpose is her own interior growth and pleasure.

If a man shows no reciprocal interest in a woman's nondomestic activities this constitutes a lack of approval even for a "healthy" woman. Approval is what it's all about in the raising of little girls—approval by the male. The fact that her husband encourages her with words to go to the symphony is all but irrelevant. His encouragement must involve some form of active participation, at least until she has been weaned off the domestic bottle. Taught since infancy to avoid spontaneous relationships with the outside world, and trained to act only when the male gives his signal, it now becomes her husband's task to deprogram her should he wish to spend his life with a growing, interesting and active human being and not with the shell of someone who spiritually passed on a few years after the wedding ceremony.

The male is ahead in the effort to remain human though

married; he leaves the playpen once a day. Yet in the critical growth area of forming and developing human relationships, of getting to know, love and respect a multitude of other human beings, he is essentially as restricted as his wife. Should he be interested in baseball and his wife is not, he can no more take out a woman friend who also enjoys baseball than can his wife go to the symphony concert with the man next door.

The fears that preclude social acceptance of such friendships revolve around fear of illicit intercourse and the growth of authentic love. The possibility of authentic love is more dreaded than illicit intercourse. The limits of sexual activity are known but nobody can control or possess the forces of interior change which love can arouse. For those who desire not the growth of their partner, but the possession and control of their partner, all relationships in which the other engages are seen as threats. This will be the case until both partners have had the chance to develop a sexually pure friendship outside the marriage.

There is no denying that friendships between sexually mature males and females is "dangerous" in the traditional moral sense. I myself do not believe in Platonic friendship; there is always an element of sexuality in mutual attraction even if the subject at hand is a baseball game. It would be absurd to close one's eyes to the realities of human drives and needs. I am not saying all friendships are basically sexual but that the other person must be compatible to one's sexuality as sexuality is part of one's totality.

Because of this element, and due to woman's traditional lack of experience in having any male relationship that was not based on the fact of her femaleness, there will be a

strong danger that many of these new male-female friendships will go sooner or later to the bedroom; hopefully,
they will not end there. The reality of this danger should
not be a deterrent. Danger, physical and moral, is part of
our daily lives; there is neither strength nor growth to be
derived from untried virtue. But there is growth and
strength to be derived from learning to love in such a way
that we enhance the dignity and strength of the other and
not destroy or devour it for one's own satisfactions. Historically, men and women both have had little opportunity to
learn to love in a disinterested fashion—to love without de-
manding an orgasm, promises, prestige, services in return.
Just to love because the uniqueness of the other's individuality has been perceived.

Marriage, excluding all loves but one, means the slow
death of the spirit to many couples who otherwise could
have had a wild fifty-year love affair with each other—
growing together, learning, making mistakes, forgiving, ex-
changing experiences and likely coming to find that this
mutual growth process has hammered out a marriage that
is endless in the depths of satisfactions offered. But most
traditional marriages appear deader than a dodo after the
first decade. It is not that the couples did not love each
other. It is that they asked, or at least expected, far too
much from one another. When satisfaction was not forth-
coming, and no opportunities were allowed in which to diffuse their intellectual and affectional needs, they died
within themselves. As human beings we are designed to
draw human nutrients from the sea of humanity around us
and to give of ourselves in return. Traditional marriage is
an aberration; it turns the couple into an isolated island.

Many of the younger feminists recognize the potentially destructive elements in the nuclear family and are refusing to marry. The ceremony itself is seen as serving a clear notice of the inherent dangers—the white of the bridal dress, the position before a sacrificial altar, the placing of a ring on the bride's finger (sometimes on the groom's), the public swearing to "love and honor," the rituals of document signing, the public nature of the reception. All declare that this relationship between two spontaneous lovers will henceforth be subservient to social considerations which will impinge upon it forcefully and frequently.

There should be little wonder that the young feminist believes that traditional marriage offers her nothing. She already has her economic independence; more companionship and a greater variety of human relationships than she could ever have within marriage; more opportunities to explore and grow at every level, physical, spiritual and intellectual. Why give it up to bind oneself in chains? Has marriage nothing to offer? Is it now obsolete?

It is likely that marriage in the sense of a lifelong union between male and female will remain; it is to be hoped that the traditional marriage will be destroyed. Those who claim that all marriage forms are obsolete are ignoring the need —particularly strong in the male—of a lifelong helpmate. They also ignore the realities of one's old age. We always think of love affairs in terms of youth and beauty, yet there is nothing in old age that precludes the total enjoyment one of the other. Indeed, if the truth could be revealed we might find that some of the greatest love affairs of our times are going on between couples in their sixties, seventies and eighties. All research indicates, furthermore, that there is nothing to prevent a couple enjoying total sexual activity right into the grave—that psychological barriers and the lack of sufficient sexual exercise in one's middle years account for the alleged impotency of the aging male. Certainly, nobody marries to insure companionship and sexual activities in one's old age, yet in an assessment of one's life these needs should not be lightly pushed aside. The need to love and be loved, to have a confidant and friend whom one can trust, becomes more critical with the passing of years. Making a lifelong commitment to another in the form of marriage does not insure anyone against the loneliness of old age but in a loving relationship it goes a long way to assuaging many of the privations of the later years.

I myself put a high price on an honorable old age; it goes on for a long, long time. And I feel that much that comes before in marriage—the fights and reconciliations, the hurts, disappointments, delights and joys—all act as the humus for mutual self-knowledge that can give a long-married couple, together in their old age, a satisfaction so deep it verges on the eternal. It goes without saying that unless the couple can grow in their early years through a network of male and female friendships the period of old age can be little better than a dog-eat-dog relationship.

The destruction of the traditional marriage will involve the creation of many new freedoms. There is no reason, for instance, why skilled women cannot work and support the family if the husband would prefer to stay home, do the housework and look after the children. There is no reason why man and wife cannot both work half-time and share equally the care of the house and children. There is no law that states that all married couples must spend every day and night of their lives together. Living arrangements should be worked out to suit the needs and temperaments of the individuals involved. Some creative temperaments are explosive; many a good marriage has been destroyed during periods of creativity when the mere presence of the other created an untenable pressure. There is nothing that states that, once married, people must settle down in one district, one state, one country, as if bound there by chains. Let everyone in total freedom work out his or her marital arrangements that will lead to the most loving and enduring growth relationship. Chances are that the passage of time would find most couples settling for a living arrangement similar to the house in the suburbs of today. But this, like fidelity, should be a choice freely taken—an exercise of *the right* to settle down and live with one's spouse in a common place of habitation. It should be a right freely chosen rather than a negative move made mandatory by marriage.

Marriage as it is presently idealized is pathological. It is a house of cards built on the foundations of human dreams and overloaded with psychological and material expectations. Nobody should shed a tear at its demise; its goals were often as base as they were unreachable. The institution of marriage in the future can be justified only if it assumes a totally new form and totally new freedoms. There is evidence that this process is already underway.

# CHAPTER

# XI

A woman who has had a baby has been exposed to the most fundamental behavior of the human as an animal. Her pubic hair is shaved off by a stranger with a razor. Her prone legs, which suddenly look albino, thick, vein-threaded and unlovely, are thrust apart by a brisk and crackling matron. A viaduct feeding what seems like gallons of hot suds is thrust up her rectum. Bent with the double pain of the impending birth and the boiling suds, the expectant mother staggers off to the toilet. There she is not even permitted the dignity of flushing.

With luck, the labor might not be too hard and either pain or drugs will dim the memory of the routine indignities that follow: the thrusting of thumbs up the rectum, the poking of fingers inside the vagina, the casual comments of the hospital staff, the tying down of one's arms and the stirruping of one's legs. Reduced to raw fecundity, one's most intimate bodily parts exposed to strangers' eyes, subjected

145

often to the yelping pain of an episiotomy, woman confronts reality.

From the loss of her virginity, through the act of conception to childbirth, woman experiences a wide spectrum of interpersonal relationships with an intensity and depth few men experience. Yet if someone says "fuck" she is supposed to leave the room. What a mountain of hypocrisy the male has imposed upon us! And what endless machinations we go through to obediently support his myths of femininity. Women, whether they have borne a child or not—biological motherhood is only one form of motherhood—are infinitely better qualified to discuss and contribute to any subject touching on humanity than the males who dominate their lives. Yet one of the prime dues demanded of women is their withdrawal from the world of free discussion. There are two reasons for this. One is that women, being "only women," could not possibly have anything of consequence to say. The second reason is more interesting. The intelligent woman has an intimate knowledge of the nature of the beast, of his needs and drives, strengths and limitations, nobility and baseness and there are few men strong enough to want that woman around. No man wants her around as a competitor.

Many males are going to suffer painful readjustments in the times ahead, for this competitive woman will appear in ever-increasing numbers. On the whole she will not wish to play the role of competitor; women are far less impressed with the gyrations necessary for material success than the system would have us believe. This competitive role will be forced upon her simply because she will have to fight for every professional inch she gets until the whole realm of

male-female relationships undergoes radical reconstruction.
There is no doubt that she will fight; facing a world that at-
tests to the failure of its male stewardship, she has no alternative. For what is it a woman sees when she looks at this,
a "man's world"? She sees a world in danger of going to
hell with good intentions. She sees the male ego walking the
international scene like the reaper of death. She sees the
male ego in the Israeli pilot who bombs a civilian factory,
or in the Arab guerrilla mining a farmer's plot, or in the
Nigerian politicians who let Biafrans starve rather than
allow in relief planes, or in American farmers who pour
milk down their drains rather than take a half-cent less, or
in Indian politicians who buy votes with people's lives.
Women cannot understand all these masculine maneuvers
and consider the grinding up of humans for the sake of
some idealistic theory unsuitable behavior even for apes.
Women love this world but the "man's world" they hold in
contempt.

It is clear, however, that the way women think or feel
about this, their world also, is of little concern. President
Richard Nixon is one who has yet to offer a shred of substantial evidence that he cares what women think or, for
that matter, that he knows they even exist, Pat, etc., excluded. Dick's attitude under analysis is one of unadulter-
ated niggerism. Of 300 presidential appointments, eight so
far have gone to women. Of 635 persons named to "Sched-
ule C" or top political posts within the federal establishment, three were women. There has been a total of eleven
other female appointments, all traditionally reserved for
women and properly known in Washington as "the ghetto
jobs." (Give or take a nigger as you read these figures; they

fluctuate slightly but the spirit remains the same.) One woman almost made it into the Urban Affairs Council which deals with inner city problems such as housing, health and illegitimacy. Only a dyed-in-the-wool Mr. Charley such as Richard Nixon could have failed to put a woman there but somehow he managed. At first he said he would; as it turned out that was not quite what he meant. An aide explained what the president had in mind: the men on the council could bring women "as aides" to the meeting. Like midwives, they would assist at the delivery of the males' mental ejaculations. Suggesting that women be aides was the tip-off on Dick, for the function of the aide is to clean up the mess somebody else has made—the traditional woman's role.

It is not necessary for women to look abroad, or even as far as Washington, D.C., to see any number of reasons why more and more females regard man's superiority as the myth of the millennium. They see, they smell, they feel, the realities—the state of the Missouri River stinking with the blood, guts and hair of slaughtered cattle; the scores of smaller rivers, yellow and thick with untreated sewerage as they crisscross the once lovely Midwestern plains; the acid pollution of Pennsylvania's streams; the near total destruction of the golden state of California; the foul death of Lake Erie and the struggle of Lake Michigan to cling to life.

The feminists are often portrayed as bitter, frustrated, frigid malcontents, as castrating bitches joined together in a sodden sisterhood of misery. And some of them are, for each feminist brings to the movement the experiences of her own life with all its frustrations and disappointments. The

majority are not, but with their bitter sisters share the same
deep anger. The essence of this anger when woman looks at
the world is the essence of her released oppression. It is not
the world in pain that inspires her wrath as much as the bitter awakening to a profound hoax—the hoax of inherent
masculine superiority. Looking back through the years of
her life, she realizes that she has been sweet, soft putty in
man's hands. She has denied her precious intelligence because of the male ego, abdicated her individuality because
of the male ego, repressed her authenticity because of the
male ego and turned her face away from her own soul because of the male ego. She has accepted employment and
remained submissive in inferior positions long after less
qualified men surged past; she has played dumb to be acceptable; pretended to sexuality out of a fictitious gratitude;
held her tongue for the sake of peace. Held her tongue not
only in good health but right down to the sometimes agonizing depths of childbirth, for is it not a male belief, hammered deep into her soul, that the pain of childbirth makes
her "a real woman"? One can only speculate as to the advances that might have been made in the realm of obstetrics
had it been men who bore the children. Has anyone ever
bothered to study the long-range psychological effects of
twelve or twenty hours of hard labor upon a young woman,
her spouse and child? This is an old saw, perhaps, but
when one observes the care taken to kill the pain of a den-
tal filling and then listens to the sounds coming from a
labor ward, one can only ask why.

Question: What is a "real woman"?

Answer: One who has been saddle broken.

Finding herself in a world that lives in the hourly realization that an atomic holocaust is a tip of a finger away, woman smells the stale misogynistic breath of those who advise her to sit and knit because "the men know what they are doing." Today, she knows too much to believe it. She knows that there is no justice without love, no love when one-third of the world goes to bed hungry, millions live on the edge of atomic despair, nations of blacks are held down by a handful of whites, and the skies of the western world turn black with soot. She knows enough to hit the bedrock of contempt when she is by-passed for a deserved promotion, when she goes through law school and ends up as a secretary, when she must work and has no place to leave her children, when she must spend milk money on buying sexual imagery such as fad clothes to hold down her job.

The Great Bugaboo of male superiority is dead. What is woman now destined to become in this world? What human characteristics will she display? What role will she assume?

We have seen that woman is no longer in bondage to her own body, that safe contraception has given her not only biological freedom but the freedom to develop an authentic morality liberated from any intimidating biological consequences. And we have seen that this freedom has come precisely at that historical moment when population growth must be held down ruthlessly because large numbers of children will not maintain the species but will destroy it.

Evidence indicates that the trend of the future will be a revolution in social attitudes towards childbearing. For centuries, reproduction was the only feminine role that was imperative and unique to the female nature. Nor do I have any doubt that if it were not for this role man would have killed off woman as a natural competitor hundreds of thousands of years ago. Now that reproduction is socially threatening, women will be able to develop a wide spectrum of other life styles. It is unlikely that the majority of women will choose to remain childless; this will take several generations of deprogramming. But it is likely that many more than in the past will choose to remain so, and others who would have borne two or three children will settle for one. There will be a smaller group who now will choose to have several children; this will be a *free* choice made by a *free* woman and not the puppetlike acting out of a socially conditioned role. From these women, who psychologically thrive on domesticity and child-raising just as other women thrive on teaching or sculpting, will come the number of children necessary for the perpetuation of the species. Let me clearly state that if the majority of women do not voluntarily choose to remain childless or limit their family to one, we are approaching a world situation in which the state will take over the licensing of the right to give birth.

What of the woman who does not have a child? She has opted out of her traditional role of mother within the present man-made social institutions; the only societally important role left to her in the present system is that of tireless consumer. To break free of this consumer role preparatory to assuming a new role will not be easy.

To reject her consumer role woman must fly in the face of some of the most powerful forces in society. She can expect no support from the male. For the male to react towards woman as mind rather than body, strength rather than weakness, substance rather than form, would involve the voluntary destruction of large parts of the social and economic system he has created, for this system is totally dependent on continually increased productivity with continually increased consumption. To woman, a nonproducer in this society and the controller of most consumer purchases, is given the power to make or break the economic system. Destruction of the present capitalistic system as we know it in the United States is no answer; with all its faults and injustices it has still provided the highest standard of living for the greatest number of peasants than any contemporary political or social system. But that it must be restructured, with women playing a major and dynamic role, is patently clear.

The question now to be asked concerns the type of role that women will most likely play. Earlier, we stated that the male image of the female as being "naturally" loving, as desiring children, as submissive, docile, soft, obedient, turned-in on self and uninterested in the wider world is sheer tripe. Some women are this way and others who are just as "female" are not. History shows that when women have been given the opportunity to defy traditional female roles because of position, wealth or politics, they have often acted in ways normally considered masculine: *e.g.,* Elizabeth I of England, Catherine the Great of Russia, author George Sand (Aurore Dupin), concentration camp commandant Ilsa Fuchs, the female Russian fighter pilots of World War II, the female combatants of the Viet Cong and the North Vietnamese Army. The conclusion drawn was that the "differences" between male and female appear to be socially conditioned and not "natural" or inborn differences—with one exception. That exception is woman's capacity to carry and bring forth life. The role that women will play will increasingly concern itself with the *quality of life*.

Life in the United States, and increasingly in Canada, Australia and most of Western Europe, is a matter of quantity. Anything that is bigger is automatically considered better—more people, more houses, bigger theaters, bigger planes, broader stationwagons, longer hotdogs, taller buildings, deeper pools, a thousand more miles of freeway. Concomitant with this orgy of quantity is more crime, more delinquency, more neglected aged, more divorce, more parentless children, more suicides, more junk, more pollution, and a totality of anxiety that pervades the nation. This emphasis on quantity in life, at the total expense of quality, is wringing out the American soul until it is dying of aridity. It is dying from lack of love; it has become one vast fictitious construct in which the tears of abandoned children, the despair of suicides, the fears of the aged, are left to be handled through the fifth-year college techniques of the twenty-two-year-old social worker. If there is a human problem, we bring in alleged skills abstracted from some empire—the educational empire, the social worker's empire, the psychiatric empire. Onto one rotten institution we impose another. We have become so frightened of our humanity, so distrustful of our reality, that we are not only alien to our brothers and neighbors, we are alien to ourselves. We talk a sociological lingo that dries no tears, impose a solution that mends no hearts, posit theories and earn doctorates that solve no problems.

This is a sick society, a society that we can reconstruct. This is not because we have been prime sufferers and know every turn of the discriminatory screw; we can reconstruct society for the best of all possible reasons—we have the brains, the brawn and the vision. This, plus a historically developed sensitivity to all values that bear on the quality of life. Our role in the future must be focused no longer on the biological bearing of our own individual young. Our skills in caring for and nuturing life must be brought into a far larger social context—the bringing to full physical, psychological and spiritual growth all the potential life forces within this society. Lest this sounds like a new switch on the old traditional role, it is emphasized that we can best accomplish social reconstruction in these terms if we enter the medical, engineering, scientific, teaching and social professions in vast numbers. Only by being in a position of corporate strength can we bring some *life values* to bear on the major decisions that affect all our lives. Until we have women in large numbers in local government, engineering and town planning we cannot hope to control the forces that destroy parks, chop up cities and lay in another 10,-000 miles of pollution-producing freeways. Until we have women in numbers researching and teaching the social sciences, we cannot hope to add an iota of hope or dignity to the welfare recipient. Until women are in politics and medicine in strength we cannot hope to tackle two of the most sensitive questions of our times—the prolongation of life for the comatose aged and for the comatose retarded whose return to consciousness is totally precluded. Although the sufferings, or the existence, of these two groups bears directly on the quality of life, open discussion on these subjects is taboo. So the aged, men and women who have led lives of dignity, are condemned to spend months and sometimes years in pain but drugged to the point where they cannot express their physical or psychological anguish. They long for a death to which their dignity as human beings entitles them. But at present there is no group in this society—which for so long has hidden death and ugliness from its consciousness—which has the courage to publicly debate what is in essence a mixture of medical-ethical gutlessness and profiteering.

As for the child who is born a helpless, total idiot—when doctors proceed as if it were a normal birth they are not confronting the question but avoiding it. This question comes to mind because I have seen cases in state mental hospitals that the average person could not, thankfully, ever imagine. Many of these lives are spent in pain, many in a continuing sleep. Grotesque though it may sound, we must ask if this adds to the quality of life either for the victim or for society. We might well decide it does; we might decide it does not. Whatever the answer, our society has reached a point where these questions must be probed and a decision taken as to whether quantity—in years kept alive, in length of freeway, height of building, etc.—is forever to take precedence over quality. Such questions, an integral part of the world of interpersonal relations, might best be answered by women.

What of the larger issues of war and international relations? When we look at the external affairs department, or the foreign affairs department, or the political affairs department, or, prime example of all, the U.S. Department of State, we see to what extent our fate lies in the hands of men. And we see that generation after generation we have war. It is not a proof of female power to force a four-dollar-a-week typing raise or to light one's own cigarettes or open a door for oneself, critical little exercises though these might appear to be. We cannot claim the achievement of power until we are in a position to stop international wars.

Over the centuries, we have acquired superb skills in negotiation and compromise; that is how we have survived. There is a bond between women internationally that does not exist between males and that is the common bond of bearing sons. It is these sons that all women sacrifice when the worst of male phallic institutions—the armed forces—goes on its generational rampage. Even when the times ahead allow few of us to bear children, we will prove to be more concerned with the preservation of human life than the preservation of theories.

In the meanwhile there is much to be done. Women who do not have a profession, or who because of other commitments or age cannot openly participate in the feminist revolution, can still make a significant contribution. Some of the ways might sound small, but it is the totality of these seemingly trivial acts that will create woman power. We must form a nationwide front to help our sisters who are employed but getting nowhere simply because they are females. We must do all in our power to help our sisters who possess superior intellectual capacities fulfill those capacities. We must watch the school system and individual teachers like hawks to ensure that our daughters will not have traditional female images imposed upon them, hence limiting their academic vision. We must close our accounts at department stores that will not open accounts for married working women without their husbands' signatures. We must let our local bank manager know just what we think of his policy of refusing credit to married working women while extending it freely to the divorced or separated woman. We can all stop shopping in stores that refuse to sell returnable bottles. We can seek out gasolines with the lowest lead and carbon content. We can walk to the store, not drive. When we go to the city we can use public transportation whenever possible. If that transportation is poor, we should raise holy hell. We should refuse to buy detergents, automatic dish-washer compounds and water conditioners until all marine life-killing phosphates have been removed. Once you catch on, the list is endless.

As we go about this hell-raising, I believe we would be well advised to take into account those few, few but suffi-cient, men who have as much understanding of the inherent injustices imposed upon women as do the movement's lead-ers. These men are of value and importance should we sin-cerely desire female liberation and not merely to raise hell. When I look at the history of the labor movement in the United States, where a bucket of blood had to be spilled to gain a drop of justice, it strikes me as verging on the schiz-ophrenic to believe that we can obtain our due by deballing every male within range. A superior guerrilla tactic is to prepare the sea through which we must swim to reach our goal. To muddy up that sea with hate is self-defeating, ther-apeutic though it might be for the individuals involved. To assume that all men are all women's enemies is to fly in the face of reality. Some of the most beautiful things that have ever happened to me as a human being happened because of male love, male generosity, male insight, male nobility and I assume this has been the experience of many women.

Instead of attempting to deball the male, I believe it more appropriate for us to become really ballsy ourselves and help myopic males understand that there is no love without liberation and no liberation without love. Then we can get on with the more important question of the quality of life, a question which relates as much to the freedom of the female as to the freedom of the male.

If we look at the world around us, we see that love has become a rare commodity, spontaneous warmth all but quenched, laughter is heard only through the television tubes. We are bound together by our humanity yet dare not look one another in the eye for fear we will see some part of ourselves reflected there, some part in need that frightens and repels us. We give our help to the unemployed in the form of a check in the mails, our help to the sick aged in the form of drugs, our help to children in the form of gadgets, our help to one another in the form of alcohol, trinkets and gestures. Why is it that we can no longer be human and love and weep and laugh and relish making fools of ourselves? For we long to do these things, we long to be more human, to put more into life, get more out of life. It is as if we are going through life on tiptoe, never really experiencing it; life passes by like a painless and bland movie when we long to sink our teeth into its being. Why can't we? What has happened to us? What has been done to us?

What has happened is simply that *our society has become one giant rational construct*. It is an intellectual abstraction and no longer relates to the warm, groping, shabby and sometimes hilarious realities of our human nature. These concepts under which we live, which force us to forever compete, to play sexually stereotyped roles, to marry as we do, raise children as we do, make war as we do, make love

as we do, work as we do and relate as we do—these concepts have polluted our souls.

We can see what has been done to our land, rivers,
beaches and forests. We can measure precisely how the face
of our planet has been polluted and partially destroyed by
false social and economic values. What is more difficult to
measure is the extent to which man's nature has been polluted and lacerated by the same kind of false social and
economic values.

The task of women in the coming decades is to ruthlessly
destroy these false constructs that dominate our life. Despite present conditions of unprecedented strain, there is all
the intelligence, goodness, strength and vision necessary to
reconstruct our entire society. The initial step has already
been undertaken—the disengagement of woman from the
historic programming of male and female roles. Once this
disengagement is completed, women of the world will be
free to tear apart all the rational constructs that do not relate to the reality of humanity.

It is no longer good enough to blame man for keeping
woman ignorant. For man himself is ignorant and in the
sum total no more capable or enlightened than woman.

Lisa Hobbs was born in Melbourne, Australia. A prize-winning reporter, she was with the San Francisco *Examiner* for ten years before joining the foreign staff of the San Francisco *Chronicle*. Lisa Hobbs is well-known as a lecturer on American college campuses and in 1967 was awarded a Professional Journalism Fellowship by the Ford Foundation to study Asian affairs at Stanford. She was a delegate to the first American Newspaper Guild National Conference on Women's Rights held in Chicago in November 1970, representing both San Francisco and Vancouver. Her first book, *I Saw Red China,* was a best seller, a book club selection and was translated into four languages. She now lives with her family on Vancouver Island.